DANCING IN A ____ R

ONE FAMILY FACES HIV/AIDS

Fritz Mutti and Etta Mae Mutti

Fritz Mutti
Etta Mae Mutti

ABINGDON PRESS

Nashville

DANCING IN A WHEELCHAIR
One Family Faces HIV/AIDS

Copyright © 2001 by Abingdon Press.

This book is printed on recycled, acid-free, elemental-chlorine–free paper.

Library of Congress Cataloging in Publication Data

Mutti, Fritz, 1938–
    Dancing in a wheelchair: one family faces HIV/AIDS / Fritz Mutti and Etta Mae Mutti.
    p. cm.
    ISBN 0-687-09805-X
    1. Mutti, Tim—Health.   2. Mutti, Fred—Health.   3. AIDS
(Disease)—Patients—United States—Biography.   4. Gay men—United States—Biography.
5. AIDS (Disease)—Religious aspects—Christianity.   I. Mutti, Etta Mae, 1938– II. title.

RC607.A26 M88 2001
362.1'969792'0092—dc21
[B]   00-065056

Unless otherwise noted, scripture quotations are from the *Good News Bible: Today's English
Version*, second edition, © 1992 by The American Bible Society.

Scripture quotations noted NRSV are from the New Revised Standard Version of the Bible,
copyright © 1989, Division of Christian Education of the National Council of the Churches
of Christ in the USA. Used by permission. All rights reserved.

Scripture quotation noted CEV is from the Contemporary English Version © 1991, 1992,
1995 by The American Bible Society. Used by permission.

03 04 05 06 07 08 09 10—10 9 8 7 6 5 4 3

MANUFACTURED IN THE UNITED STATES OF AMERICA

This book is dedicated to the memory of Tim and Fred Mutti, whose lives will always be intertwined with all those who knew them. Their courage in the face of an early death provided an example for us to follow. The unwavering faith that they exhibited helped us examine our own faith and become stronger Christians. The love they expressed for their family and friends was a reason for celebration and created a desire for all concerned to extend that love to others.

This book is also dedicated to their brother, Marty, who shows us all how fun life can be. He has taken on the role of only son with dignity and courage and has grown in compassion, understanding, and awareness of the hurts of others. His sense of humor keeps us laughing, and his strength encourages us day by day.

CONTENTS

Foreword 7

Preface 9

Introduction 11

Chapter 1   Eyes of Death 13

Chapter 2   High School Sweethearts 17

Chapter 3   Ordinary Happiness 19

Chapter 4   The Bad News 27

Chapter 5   HIV/AIDS 101 31

Chapter 6   A Burden Too Heavy 37

Chapter 7   Learning to Live with HIV/AIDS 43

Chapter 8   The Hard Task of Telling Others 47

Chapter 9   Four Months to Live 51

Chapter 10   Went to Alaska 61

Chapter 11   Dancing in a Wheelchair 65

Chapter 12   Trapped by AIDS 67

Chapter 13   Two Hospitalizations at the Same Time 71

Chapter 14   "I'm Ready to Die" 77

Chapter 15   "I'm Dying" 81

Chapter 16   Celebrating Death and Resurrection 85

Chapter 17   A Family in Mourning 89

Chapter 18   Moving to Florida 95

Chapter 19   Another Son's Death 99

Chapter 20   Celebrating Death and Resurrection II 103

Chapter 21   Friends Care 107

Chapter 22   In Memory Of 111

Chapter 23   The Mutti AIDS Fund 115

Chapter 24   Life Stories in Three-by-Six Panels 117

Chapter 25   The Struggle Against Judgment and Hatred . . 121

Chapter 26   Facing Life Through Faith 127

FOREWORD

When Fritz Mutti and Etta Mae Mutti asked me to write a foreword to their new book, *Dancing in a Wheelchair,* I accepted without hesitation. I did so because of my admiration and appreciation for Etta Mae and Fritz over the years. My colleague and mentor, Bishop W. T. Handy, Jr., used to speak of Fritz and Etta Mae with profound affection and respect. Also, Fritz and I were among the fifteen bishops at Denver in 1996 who called on The United Methodist Church to be open to all persons, especially gays and lesbians.

Because of my own journey with grief with the death of my spouse and the need to complete my Renewal Leave in 1999, I could not find the time to read the manuscript until Martin Luther King Jr. Day 2000. What a surprise! I started reading and could not stop. I read the whole manuscript in one sitting.

This book is a powerful testimony of a couple who lived out the experience of HIV/AIDS through the lives of their two sons, Tim and Fred, who were gay. What a story! It is a labor of love. It flames the emotions of shame, fear, hate, and love. It challenges one's faith beliefs. It confirms the assurance that God, through Jesus Christ, enables persons to overcome the unimaginable situations and circumstances of life.

I am proud to recommend this book as necessary reading for those who are struggling to understand the issue of homosexuality. It will be instructive to a parent whose child is gay or lesbian. It will provide spiritual insights for people of faith who are seeking greater biblical understanding. It will challenge the typical myths regarding persons who are gay or lesbian.

I am grateful to Etta Mae and Fritz for their willingness to allow themselves to be vulnerable by addressing this controversial subject of homosexuality. I predict this book will make a significant contribution to the continuing debate on the role and place of gays and lesbians in our churches and in society as a whole.

> Melvin G. Talbert
> January 17, 2000
> Retired Bishop
> The United Methodist Church

PREFACE

Stories come in different forms. This one arises from our personal experience as a family living with HIV/AIDS. We lived it. We continue to live it. We have told this story orally in hundreds of intimate conversations, and in dozens of workshops, seminars, and conferences. On one of those occasions, our friend Don Messer heard our presentation. "You need to publish that story," he encouraged. "Your story needs to be heard by many people. It puts a face on HIV/AIDS."

We confessed that we had considered the possibility. Already we had put the story on paper in a few articles and other contributions to publications. But another book did not seem necessary. Surely there were enough publications available already. Two of the most helpful resources were written by persons who have become our friends as we shared each other's stories of grief and hope. One of those books is *The Walking Wounded* by Beverly Barbo; the other, by Beverly Cole, is titled *Cleaning Closets: A Mother's Story.*[*]

Don Messer urged us to undertake the project anyway. "Your story is uniquely yours. It is different from other stories, and it includes content that will be helpful to many." Finally we gave in to our friend's prompting.

As we began the first draft, it became clear that a written document could not have the same personal dimension that we express in oral presentations. In an effort to maintain some of the personal dimension, however, we have chosen to use a dialogical format. We have tried to put the story on the page in much the same way we could offer it in a face-to-face setting. We designate which one of us is speaking by the use of our names: Etta Mae for the mother, Fritz for the father. We also may provide reflective paragraphs or helpful quotations as a means of connecting our experience with larger concerns.

This manuscript represents a labor of love that has benefited us. The writing has been hard work, but the personal blessings are genuine. We hope that *Dancing in a Wheelchair* will be a blessing to our readers as well.

* Beverly Foote Barbo, *The Walking Wounded* (Lindsborg, Kansas: Carlsons' Publishing, 1987); Beverly Cole, *Cleaning Closets: A Mother's Story* (St. Louis: Chalice Press, 1995).

INTRODUCTION

The global health crisis, HIV/AIDS, produces staggering numbers. Millions of adults around the world live with the killer virus that attacks the human immune system and leaves them defenseless against a raft of opportunistic diseases.

In the United States, about one million people are currently infected with the virus that causes AIDS. Most of these persons have not reached their fiftieth birthday. A large number do not know they are infected, because they have not exhibited any of the symptoms.

In spite of these overwhelming statistics, many people believe that HIV/AIDS is not a problem where they live. They view it as someone else's concern. They consider the risk level minimal and the medical warnings as alarmist.

Some, who acknowledge the reality, blame those who are sick. They conclude that those who suffer deserve it because their decisions were bad and their lifestyles are immoral. They oppose funding for medical research, and they block caring ministries for those living with the virus.

Every year, however, thousands of people die of AIDS-related illnesses. Real persons suffer and die. Each one who dies is someone's son or daughter, mother or father, spouse, fellow worker, or social acquaintance. Each one has a face. Each one has a story.

These pages tell of our family's journey with HIV/AIDS. We try to make it a personal story, a human story, a spiritual story. We want to show faces and share events that reveal our humanity and vulnerability. We pray that our openness will enable many to learn, grow, change, and care.

1

EYES OF DEATH

Etta Mae: We were married in the summer of 1959, before Fritz's senior year of college. After five years of courting, we thought we were ready!

Right away I became pregnant! Nine months and two days after our wedding our first son, Tim, was born on March 9, 1960. This wasn't how we had planned to order our lives—by starting a family immediately. Since Fritz had one more year of college, it seemed important to us that I get a job and provide the income for us. Therefore, I had planned on interviewing for a job right before Fritz started school. However, we decided it would not be fair to an employer to have me begin a job, then announce that I was pregnant. So we decided just to survive on the income from Fritz's work as the student pastor of three small-membership Methodist churches. As we remember it the annual salary was $2,200. Surprisingly, we seemed to have enough money to eat well and pay the rent—two very important items!

Tim was three months old when we loaded up the trailer and moved to Evanston, Illinois, so Fritz could start seminary. Tim was a cute baby, and our neighbors fell in love with him right away. With Tim as a conversation starter it was easy for us to make many new friendships.

When Tim was two and a half years old, another unplanned baby came along. Fred was born on August 12, 1962, at Evanston

Hospital, and his life doubled our pleasure. Fred entered this life with a large birthmark on his forehead, and while he was still a tiny baby we decided to have it removed. We marvel now at the fact that the plastic surgeon performed the operation without charge to us because we were struggling seminary students with very little money.

One weekend, just a few weeks later, when Fred was about six months old, he became ill. Vomiting and diarrhea went on long enough for us to become concerned so we called our pediatrician. She was away for the weekend; another doctor was on call. He listened to us describe Fred's symptoms and then suggested we give him a little paregoric and plenty of liquids. He thought Fred would get better soon. I called that doctor off and on several times that day, and he kept assuring me that everything would be all right. He evidently had great confidence in the medicine he prescribed.

Fritz: At that time, I was serving a student pastorate at the Methodist church in Leroy, Indiana. It was about an hour's drive to the church. Should I go and assume my Sunday responsibilities? We agreed that it would be all right since we had assurances from the doctor that we need not worry about Fred's condition. I did wait until Sunday morning to go, rather than making our usual Saturday morning trek.

Etta Mae: After Fritz left for the church, Fred continued to exhibit the same symptoms. I stayed in touch with the doctor, who felt there was no reason for alarm. I recall, however, that Fred didn't sleep. He didn't cry, he just didn't sleep. I would go check on him in his crib, and he would be lying there quietly with his big brown eyes open, not complaining, but telling me without words that he hurt.

On Sunday afternoon our pediatrician returned to the city. She checked her calls at the office, saw how many times I had called her colleague, and decided to make a house call on Fred. I could see the concern in her eyes as she examined him. She finished her exam quickly and called the hospital, arranging for his admission. "We have a very sick boy here," she said. "He is terribly dehydrated, and we need to get him to the hospital right away." The hospital told her they didn't have any beds available, and I can still hear her say, "Find one! This baby is coming in!"

I asked our friends next door to look after Tim. While I was making arrangements for Tim's care, Dr. Jones forced water down Fred's throat with a spoon in order to get liquids down him. He just looked at her, again without complaining, and tried his best to swallow. Dr. Jones then loaded Fred and me into her car and took us to the hospital.

Fritz: Etta Mae got in touch with me through church members, and I left Leroy immediately and headed for Evanston Hospital. When I got there, our baby boy was on the critical list. We didn't know what to do, so we held hands and waited in helpless silence. We were young, naïve, and very inexperienced. Even so, we knew that Fred's eyes had the look of death. We were dismayed and alone. We weren't much good at prayer, but we found the chapel and offered our simple request for God's gift of healing. I did not cry, but the lump in my throat made it nearly impossible to speak.

Etta Mae: My tears started the instant I saw Fritz. Release had come for me in that form, but the scared and lonely feeling remained. Fred's veins had collapsed, and the only place the doctor could find a vein that was still slightly inflated was in Fred's ankle. The needle was inserted there, and the liquid began to drip into his body. The slow movement toward recovery began.

Fritz: After a few hours of this steady drip of liquid into Fred's body, he began to improve. He took on some color. His eyes regained some of their sparkle. We could urge a smile from him occasionally now. Our little baby was getting well, and we could begin anticipating a full recovery.

It was a terrible experience. We thought it would be the worst experience we would ever have to face. It was not.

2

HIGH SCHOOL SWEETHEARTS

Fritz: We grew up in the small northwest Missouri community of Hopkins. It had a population of about 750 souls. My dad owned and operated an automobile dealership. Mom was a schoolteacher by training, but she never took a teaching position after she and dad were married.

I grew up in a loving, secure family. World War II brought an end to the Great Depression, and the 1940s and 1950s were stable times for rearing a family. From my childhood, I remember many pleasant experiences. My sister, Sue, and I enjoyed hours of playing together. The family went to Sunday school and worship together nearly every week. In the summer, we took wonderful vacation trips to Colorado, Yellowstone National Park, California, and Banff National Park in Canada.

I liked school. Good teachers helped me learn and excel in my studies. Coaches invited me to try my hand at every sport, and music teachers taught me to read music and enjoy the fine arts, even though I was a poor piano student and not much better on the baritone horn.

Those formative years put my life on a solid foundation.

Etta Mae: All of my growing-up years, including high school, were spent on a farm. My dad farmed eighty acres in order to make a living for his family of eight. (In 1999, highway signs said one farmer feeds 128 people!) We lived ten miles from Hopkins,

Missouri, where Fritz and I attended high school together. When I was sixteen years old, my mother and father announced that we would be moving that spring as the farm we lived on was being sold. Fritz and I had just been dating a few months and I wasn't sure of our relationship; thus, my fear was that when my family moved to another town, our dating days would end. Luckily, that didn't happen. We stayed in the Hopkins community, Fritz and I continued to date, fell in love, and committed ourselves to each other.

My mother and dad took us to the Disciples of Christ church to Sunday school and worship with regularity. My home life was a secure one, although we were never financially well off. I was a wanted child, I was given a solid foundation on which to form my values, I was the first daughter, after two sons, and I was loved. My parents were completely devoted to each other; and my brothers, my sister, and I experienced that devotion every day of our lives.

I had a close relationship with my mother, who always let it be known I could tell or ask her anything. And I did! That relationship continued into adulthood, and she was the first one I would go to for sharing. I was determined I would nourish that kind of relationship with my own children. However, as you will discover later, there are just some things that are not told easily to a parent. My mother died in August 1999, and the loss of the relationship I had with her will never be overcome.

3

ORDINARY HAPPINESS

Don't break off contact; don't reject your child. A shocking number of homosexual youth end up on the streets because of rejection by their families. This and other external pressures can place young people at greater risk of self-destructive behaviors like substance abuse and suicide.

*Your child may need you and the family now more than ever. He or she is still the same person. This child, who has always been God's gift to you, may now be the cause of another gift: your family becoming more honest, respectful and supportive. Yes, your love can be tested by this reality, but it can also grow stronger through your struggle to respond loving.**

Fritz: During adolescence all of us begin work on very important questions. One of those questions centers on the matter of intimacy. Will I find someone who will be my life partner? After Etta Mae and I decided to join our lives in marriage, a core commitment and value was established that would affect everything else in our experience. We would live our lives together in pursuit of happiness, fulfillment, and meaning.

Etta Mae: The covenant we made aimed toward a life of shared love and support. We wanted nothing grandiose—just ordinary happiness.

After graduation from high school, I worked a year to raise funds to attend college. At the end of my sophomore year, we decided to marry. I would work while Fritz finished his schooling. It seemed like a manageable plan. Just an ordinary happiness is what we wanted.

Fritz: Our marriage covenant was closely connected to my vocational covenant. During our high school years, the Cold War pitted two world superpowers and their allies against each other. The United States of America and the Union of Soviet Socialist Republics tried to outstrip each other in military might. The nuclear competition put the entire globe in danger. At a critical time in this deadly competition, one of the monumental events of world history took place. The Soviet Union launched a rocket into space. Human beings no longer were earth bound.

American pride was severely wounded, and the call went out for a patriotic response. As Uncle Sam had called for volunteers to enlist in the war effort a decade earlier, now the nation sought to enlist scientists and engineers in the space race. Etta Mae and I graduated from high school in the spring of 1956, just as this plea was in full sway. I had always liked math and science and decided I would respond by studying for a degree in aeronautical engineering. I enrolled at Iowa State University and started toward that goal.

It was a rocky road. I was a small-town kid ill equipped for life in a large university. There were twenty-six seniors in our high-school class. A chemistry lecture at Iowa State had almost as many students as my hometown had residents. In high school I always made excellent grades. In college I did not do well. I was embarrassed, frightened, and discouraged. When I went to my professors for help they told me to work harder.

Something else was working on me. In 1953 or 1954, my father began to experience health problems. He found it difficult to maintain his balance. He could not pick up silverware with either hand. He lost weight. Dad and Mom went to the famed Mayo Clinic in Rochester, Minnesota, in 1954 and came home with a devastating diagnosis. Dad had amyotropic lateral sclerosis, often identified as Lou Gehrig's Disease after the great baseball player who died from it. ALS is an incurable disease. It took Dad's life when he was only forty-seven years of age.

Up against the realities of life and death, I began to ask questions about the meaning of life. Every inquiry took me to my religious training in search of answers. Through this struggle, I sensed that God was moving me toward a new vocational commitment. I felt that God was calling me to the life of a pastor in the church. I concluded that working with people would be much more important than building rockets. This trial ended in submission and redirection. I said yes to the call to the ministry and began a new journey.

In preparation for life as an ordained minister, I transferred to Central Methodist College, Fayette, Missouri, and completed my degree there. My seminary degree came from Garrett-Evangelical Theological Seminary in Evanston, Illinois. Student pastorates during college and seminary confirmed my calling and provided a meager income to support us.

Etta Mae: As that first pregnancy (with Tim) made taking a job impractical in Fayette, it also proved true at seminary. After moving to Evanston, I did contract typing for Northwestern University students, and I provided day care for two other small children. When Fritz began full-time pastoral ministry in a church after graduation from seminary, major attention was given to the task of parenting. At the end of our first full-time pastorate we were blessed with our third son, Marty. He was born on March 9, 1965, and grew up to fit the description of a third child perfectly—friendly, easy-going, lots of friends, and an easy child to parent. He also came into the world with red hair and a few freckles, something he was teased about by acquaintances. However, he took it in stride, being proud of his hair, and telling people he had acquired it from his Grandma Mutti's red shoes! Life was hectic, but our hopes began unfolding as planned.

Fritz: During the elementary school years, Tim and Fred had different interests than other boys. They liked music and art and hated sports. They excelled in academic pursuits. They enjoyed playing with girls rather than boys.

The other boys picked on them and called them sissies. Some days the school bullies chased Tim home after school. On several other occasions they pestered him and made fun of him. This took place in a small, rural town in Missouri where I was the pastor of a church. Tim would find refuge from the chasing by running into the church to my office on his way home. We didn't report this harassment, since we knew nothing would be done about it. But we discussed it with Tim and Fred and encouraged them not to provoke these other boys, to try their best to get along with them.

This was the beginning of what would result in their exclusion from certain groups.

Etta Mae: We were concerned about the reaction other boys had to our sons so we took them to a counselor and expressed our suspicions about their sexual orientation. This was in the late 1960s, a time when discussions of this nature were not common. We didn't know much about homosexuality—only the stereotypes and the myths and the prejudices.

Fritz: We were relieved when the counselor told us not to worry about Tim and Fred. He assured us they would grow up to be fine young men, and they did.

So did Marty. Throughout his years of development he fit the stereotype of the all-American boy. He loved sports and excelled in baseball and basketball. He made others laugh. Everyone liked him, and he showed a natural ability to lead. Our house was the gathering place for all his friends.

Etta Mae: So during these years of parenting we worried about the normal experiences of adolescence. We endured their rebellious years by watching them test their wings and strive for independence. They were determined not to act like "preacher's kids," so they purposely chose activities that "religious" people didn't take part in. We got impatient with them during their senior years in high school. We gritted our teeth and didn't ask many questions when they went off to college to experiment with life. All three of our sons were good students. Tim had graduated co-valedictorian of his high-school class, and Fred graduated with a 3.7 grade point average on a 4.0 scale. Both were very musical, singing in select choruses and accompanying soloists for music contests. We didn't want to see those talents go to waste and encouraged them in their pursuit of careers in the world of arts.

Fritz: Marty did well academically also, but he stressed sports and relationships rather than academics. He excelled there and still loves to watch and participate. Marty tried piano lessons at a young age, but it just didn't hold his interest. He did play in the school band while he was in junior high and high school, but would much rather have been out on the baseball field. Even though he didn't have much of an interest in music and art, his relationship with Tim and Fred was very good. At times when Tim and Fred were in competition and appeared to wish they were not brothers, Marty was the stabilizing force among them and would always be able to keep life on a even keel. We did discover, however, many years later, that Tim and Fred had collaborated on a plan to have Marty locked in a closet, bound and gagged, just to keep him out of their way. Even when that happened, Marty was not offended; he certainly didn't want us to know, so he didn't reveal it to us for a long time. When all three were together and talking about it, there was lots of laughter surrounding the event, even from Marty.

After the boys were adults and had been on their own for a while, Marty raised anew the suspicions that we had voiced when Tim and Fred were in grade school. "Some of my friends at school say that Fred is gay," he reported to us. Our old fears returned, and we agonized about a course of action. Should we approach Fred about his orientation or wait for him to tell us? After several months, we decided we wanted to know definitely. When we put the question to Fred directly, he immediately disclosed the truth he had been living with. He said he had wanted to tell us sooner, but he was afraid. Somehow he thought we would not love him if we knew he was gay.

Etta Mae: We assured him we would always love him. "You are the same person you have always been, Fred, and we have suspected your sexual orientation for many years." He then said to us: "You can't possibly know how relieved I am right now. I have been hiding a very important part of my life from you, and now I am free to tell you everything that I am doing and who I am. I can share my joys with you when I date someone special and I can come to you for comfort when relationships don't work out."

Fritz: Fred told us he thought Tim was gay too. We discovered later that the two had discussed their orientation with each other but not with us. Fred not only *thought* Tim was gay, he knew it from Tim's self-disclosure. He didn't feel free to completely share the fact, but he was encouraging us to approach Tim, also. This discussion took place one evening when both boys were home. As we talked with Fred, Tim walked past the bedroom door and we invited him to join our conversation with Fred, but he was not willing to do so.

Several months later Tim wrote us a letter. In it he told of his struggle to be straight. "I wanted to be like almost everyone else. I didn't want to be gay," he wrote. "Too many negative things happen to gay people so I prayed that God would make me straight, but nothing happened. I have now begun to accept myself as a gay man and I hope you will accept me, too."

Etta Mae: In the middle of the night, after getting Tim's letter, I went to the bathroom off the kitchen, where Fritz wouldn't hear me, and began to sob. I moaned, I muffled my sobs, and I cried aloud so God would hear me. Had I done something wrong to have *two* sons who were gay? Was it environment, after all, that caused it? Was it Fritz's fault? How would the boys be treated by others once it was public? What would their lives be like? How much pain would they suffer because of who they were? Many thoughts went through my head, mostly thoughts about how much society would cause them to miss out on. I was thinking not only of how society would treat our sons, but also of what our friends and acquaintances in the United Methodist Church would do to them and to us. I wondered if they would even allow *us* to stay in the church, and I knew for certain that Tim and Fred would be isolated and encouraged to leave our denomination. These were our sons and we knew the church did not approve of them—not because of something they had done but because of who they were. How do a mother and father handle that without becoming bitter? We didn't know at this time how that would happen, or if it would.

Like Fred, Tim had been afraid to risk losing our love and acceptance. He voiced that concern to us when we called him to say we had gotten his letter. I said, "How could you possibly think we wouldn't love or accept you? Don't you know how much you are loved?" He said: "Mom, I have had friend after friend who thought their parents would accept them with open arms, but when they told their parents about their sexuality, they were disowned and thrown out of their homes. I just didn't want to take that chance. I love you both too much to not have you in my life."

Sometime later Tim wrote to his grandmothers about his self-awareness. We came across a copy after my mother died and the family was sorting through her belongings. In that letter he wrote:

... I am fairly offended that I even have to do this since I usually spend most of my energy trying to convince the other person that I am not some kind of warped psychotic. No one would ever expect a heterosexual person to defend himself or herself in the same way. However, our society has set the rules in such a way that I have no choice except to argue against them.

I do not know why I am gay. Nor do I really care since I have no intention of trying to change my sexuality. I am more concerned about learning to love myself just as I am and about finding ways to use my sexuality constructively. *I do know that I am not gay because I chose to be that way.* (Italics added.) I did not sit down and measure the alternative of homosexuality versus heterosexuality. . . .

On the other hand, I did make a choice of sorts—a choice to accept who I am. That was one of the most difficult things I have ever done. I knew that if I decided to be true to my created self, I would have an extremely rough life ahead. I would be chastised, rejected, labeled with untruths, verbally and physically abused, and forbidden to continue in the church (United Methodist) or working with children. As I find the strength to become more and more open about my gayness, I am learning that all these fears are very real possibilities. Nevertheless, the suffering that comes from the injustices other people inflict upon me is minimal compared to the suffering of trying to be straight (which I guess is also something that other people had forced me to do). . . .

You have probably heard the following things: gay men hate women; gay men wish they were women; gay men are so unattractive that women won't have them; gay men are child molesters; gay men sleep with hundreds of other men each year (or month, or week, or night); gay men all have AIDS. Some of those things are true about some gay men, but by-and-large, they are all inaccuracies. I, for example, do not fall into any of those categories. I strongly suspect that such rumors get started by straight people who are insecure about their own sexuality.

Probably the most pressing issue for me is my future relationship with the church. . . . Feminists have helped me learn how to read the Bible carefully enough to discover what it is really saying. . . .

25

It seems the real reason God destroyed Sodom was because of inhospitality. (Incidentally, sodomy laws in our country apply to heterosexual sex—including oral sex—too, although they have not been enforced against straights). . . .

Fritz: We struggled desperately with this new reality of two gay sons. We wanted an ordinary happiness. We wanted the boys to grow up like other young people, find the right vocational choices, and live their lives with satisfaction.

One time, years later, I mentioned this to colleagues. "We just wanted normal lives," I said, "just an ordinary happiness." And they replied, "Fritz, nothing is `normal.' "

Tim even said to us once, "This means I won't be giving you any grandchildren." That seemed so minor to us, but evidently it was a concern of Tim's. We just wanted him to be happy.

Etta Mae: We knew that true openness about homosexuality invited hatred and rejection. So we waited a long time before we told anyone besides our mothers. Our first disclosure was to two couples, our closest friends. They supported us and surrounded us with love, just as we knew they would.

Fritz: We told no one in our churches. That would have generated a firestorm of rejection and hostility from too many folks. It was safer to trust only a few with our knowledge.

We did seek help from a family counselor. In the first session we mustered up enough nerve to talk about homosexuality. The therapist's immediate response had nothing to do with our acceptance of our sons' sexual orientations. Instead she gasped, "Aren't you afraid of AIDS?"

Etta Mae: Right then we were not afraid of AIDS. We should have been.

* From "Always Our Children: A Pastoral Message to Parents of Homosexual Children and Suggestions for Pastoral Ministers" by the National Conference of Catholic Bishops, September 10, 1997.

4

THE BAD NEWS

I ASK FOR YOUR AWARENESS

*You may know me: you may not. I might be your friend
or perhaps we have never met. I do not ask for your pity
or sympathy, nor on the other hand, do I ask for your
judgment or condemnation. All I ask for is your awareness. Your awareness so that we can stop the spread of
this senseless disease. Your awareness so that we can help
support those that need someone to turn to, and your
awareness to help protect you and your family from the
grief that this plague brings with it. . . .*

*Those that journey through the fiery bowels of this dis-
ease are not only the ones who have contracted the virus.
There are also the spouses, family members and friends.
These are the people that must learn to live with the fact
that their loved one is living on borrowed time.*

*Many of these spouses, family members and friends do
learn to continue their lives, yet choose to do so with one
exclusion: their loved one. Hundreds of infected people are
not only taking this dismal journey alone, they must die
alone because of ignorance and misinformation. A husband with a heart disease we choose to pamper. A sister
with cancer, we choose to spoil. However, a son with AIDS,
too many fathers choose to disown. A friend with
AIDS, too many people choose to judge. A worker
with AIDS, too many employers choose to terminate. And
a child with AIDS, too many people choose to ignore.*[*]

Etta Mae: In December of 1988, Fred called to tell us that he was
in the hospital. When we asked what was wrong, he told us he had

pneumonia. He said they were running tests to find out what kind of pneumonia he had.

We wonder now why no red flags went up for us. Why would a twenty-six-year-old man have pneumonia? We passed it off. After all, Fred had always been susceptible to respiratory illness. Ever since that hospitalization as an infant, his resistance to colds and flu seemed low.

Fred called us a couple of days later to say the test results were back and that he had *Pneumocystis carinii* pneumonia (PCP). We were unfamiliar with that term and had to ask what it was. "It is the AIDS pneumonia," he replied. We were stunned. We did not even know that he was HIV-positive.

Fritz: He told us that he had known for about a year that he was infected. They discovered it when he volunteered to give blood for a drive at his place of employment. He had not informed us because he knew we would worry a lot.

Of course, we would have worried ourselves sick. More important, we hated the idea that we had not been able to help him carry the burden. For a year he had lived with the illness, wondering each time he got sick if it were a symptom of AIDS.

Etta Mae: We remember distinctly the night he called with the bad news. It was around 5:30, and we were expecting dinner guests at 6:00. As we hung up the phone after talking to Fred, I said to Fritz, "Don't say a word. I can't discuss this right now or I will go to pieces." So we put on our "happy masks" and went right ahead and entertained our guests. The minute the door was closed behind them, we both fell apart.

Fritz: My first thought at hearing the news that Fred had AIDS was "Fred is going to die."

Etta Mae: I don't remember thinking that. In fact, I kept an optimistic view throughout. Somehow I *knew* that a cure was right around the corner and it would come in time to heal Fred. Fritz kept me realistic for the next three years, and I kept him hopeful.

In April of 1989 we were hit with more bad news in a letter from Tim. It was hard for him to tell us bad news over the phone; perhaps it is hard for most of us to tell bad news over the phone. He wrote to tell us that he had been tested for AIDS. The results had just come back with the news that this twenty-nine-year-old son of ours was HIV-positive.

How could we bear the fact that another son might be dead before he reached his thirtieth birthday? How could Tim accept this, knowing exactly what was in store for him? How could our family endure this? Would we lose two of our three sons? What in the world had we done to deserve this? Why do some families seem to go through life unscathed and we were hit so hard? Couldn't life deal with us more fairly?

Fritz: During the year before Tim was diagnosed, he had worked for AID Atlanta. He knew exactly want it meant to be a Person Living with AIDS. He had cared for those persons living with AIDS, written about them in seminary papers at Candler School of Theology, dealt with legal issues with them, watched them die. Now he was facing a life like theirs.

---

* From our friend Kip Weiner, one of the first Jewish young men to reveal publicly that he was living with AIDS. This quotation appeared in the *National Jewish Post and Opinion*.

5

HIV/AIDS 101

As the HIV/AIDS pandemic rapidly encircled the globe in the
1980s, a variety of responses ensued:

Huge numbers of people recoiled in fear. Some panic occurred.
Thousands of people were sick and dying, and the medical community knew too little about the virus and how it spread. It is not
surprising that anxiety levels rose to a fever pitch.

Myths took over and rumors spread: You get AIDS from the air.
Mosquitos pass the virus. Infected persons spread the virus
through handshakes, sneezes, social kisses, touching doorknobs,
swimming in public pools. Unsuspecting persons could acquire
HIV from towels, bed linens, dishes, or hot tubs.

Frightened leaders proposed quick fixes too, such as mandatory
testing for the virus among all hospital patients as well as those
applying for marriage licenses. A longer-range cure proposal
called for a required curriculum in every public school.

Blaming and hatred arose out of that fear. Well-known television
evangelists observed that gay men were the largest group infected
in the United States. Intravenous drug users also had a high inci-
dence of infection. Since those infected were considered immoral
by the preachers, judgment came easily. This illness, they wailed,
must be God's punishment on sinners.

The hysteria created the modern equivalent of biblical leprosy.
Those living with AIDS were labeled "unclean" and regarded as

"outcasts," and, literally, "untouchable." Their presence at work, at school, in the homes of their families, and even in hospitals became intolerable.

Fritz: In those years, before we knew Tim and Fred were infected with HIV/AIDS, I was a director of the General Board of Discipleship of The United Methodist Church. That body knew that the church needed to respond in some way. Since education was one of four major responsibilities, the Board published a very helpful booklet, *AIDS and the Ministry of the Church,* by R. Michael Casto. It proved to be a very useful study guide to help congregations develop a compassionate plan for action. It is still relevant more than a decade after its first publication.

At the Missouri West Annual Conference in 1986, I introduced the following resolution:

> In recent years, a new, ugly and dangerous disease called AIDS (Acquired Immune Deficiency Syndrome) has appeared in many countries of the world. Those who contract the disease suffer devastating illness which, most frequently, ends in death. Those who suffer from AIDS, as well as family members and loved ones, experience additional psychological trauma because of fear and rejection by the general population.
>
> We, the members of the Missouri West Annual Conference of The United Methodist Church, recognize the centrality of healing ministries and pastoral care in the life of the church. We applaud those local United Methodist churches which have already undertaken special ministries in the midst of the AIDS epidemic. We urge all churches of the conference to (1) accept persons in their illness and offer them God's healing grace; (2) pray for persons with AIDS; (3) seek understanding of the disease through study which utilizes resources of the medical community and the general church (such as materials being prepared by the General Agencies); (4) engage in theological reflection of the ministry of healing.

The legislative committee handling the resolution added an amendment calling on the conference to "recognize that the major avenues of spreading AIDS are promiscuous homosexual activity and illegal intravenous drug use, condemn those practices and work to halt them as the best means of slowing this epidemic." In the debate on the issues, I moved that the amendment be stricken, arguing that the amendment reversed the intent of the resolution. To adopt the amendment would send a message of judgment and hostility, rather than one of compassion and grace. In the end the conference concurred with my plea, but it was clear now that the development of meaningful ministry to and with persons living with AIDS would be a very difficult task.

In 1987, The United Methodist Church held a national consultation on AIDS ministries in the San Francisco suburb of Millbrae. The purpose of the consultation was to "enable persons from local churches and annual conferences to develop visible ministries in compassionate and hope-filled response to the theological, spiritual, social and medical challenges of AIDS."

I attended this conference, and during the course of the event I received much information; more important, I met persons who were living with AIDS. In spite of their emaciated appearances, each one conveyed a spirit of hope and compassion. Each one gave a face to AIDS. These opportunities taught me much about HIV/AIDS. They led me into personal relationship with persons living with AIDS and moved me to specific actions in advocacy.

All these experiences took place, however, before I knew that two of our sons were infected by HIV. When the pandemic became our personal ordeal, everything took on a new appearance.

We knew that we needed a basic course in AIDS 101. Tim and Fred were our primary teachers. We also attended several different workshops. Over time we came to work from the following outline:

HIV/AIDS 101
DEFINITIONS

1. What is AIDS?	The acronym describes it:
ACQUIRED	one must become infected
IMMUNE	refers to body's natural defenses
DEFICIENCY	indicates immune system is not functioning normally
SYNDROME	refers to the various symptoms that arise when immune system is impaired

2. What is the cause of AIDS?

HIV—human immunodeficiency virus. The virus attacks the human immune system and weakens that system until infections and cancers cannot be warded off.

HOW IS HIV/AIDS TRANSMITTED?

1. Intimate sexual contact

Although the AIDS virus is found in several body fluids, a person acquires the virus during sexual contact with an infected person's blood or semen or vaginal secretions. The virus then enters a person's bloodstream through the vagina, penis, or rectum.

2. Intravenous drug use

The virus is carried in contaminated blood left in the needle, syringe, or other drug-related implements, and the virus is injected into the new victim by reusing dirty syringes and needles.

3. Mother to fetus

An infected mother transmits the virus to the fetus. Present treatment methods show some success in treating the baby while still in the womb. The baby, in some cases, will not be infected with the virus when it is born.

4. Blood transfusion

In the early years blood supplies sometimes got contaminated. Ryan White, a youth, received tainted blood through a transfusion, and his case led to the development of procedures to assure pure blood supplies. This way of transmission is almost nonexistent at the present time with the excellent screening of blood when it is received.

NON-TRANSMISSION

AIDS is not spread by common everyday contact. Shaking hands, hugging, social kissing, crying, coughing, or sneezing will not transmit HIV. Nor has AIDS been contracted from swimming in pools or bathing in hot tubs or from eating in restaurants. AIDS is not contracted from sharing bed linens, towels, cups, straws, dishes, or any other eating utensils. You cannot get AIDS from toilets, doorknobs, telephones, office machinery, or household furniture. Neither insects nor pets transmit HIV.

PREVENTION

1. Abstinence is the surest way of prevention. Avoid the high-risk behaviors and you will not get HIV/AIDS.

2. Monogamy. Having sex with more than one partner is never a good thing. With HIV loose in the world, taking chances with several persons can kill you.

3. Condoms, while not totally reliable, reduce the risk of sexual transmission by reducing the likelihood of mixing body fluids.

RISK FACTORS

1. Sexual activity with more than one trusted person is a risk factor. When persons have multiple sexual partners it is very difficult to know much about those partners' past behavior. They may carry the virus and not even know it. Abstinence is the one sure safeguard. Monogamy usually assures knowledge of your partner's behavior.

2. Illicit drug use is dangerous business. A very high number of infected persons have engaged in the risky practice of sharing dirty needles.

3. Having a sexual partner who is engaged in high-risk activity puts you in danger. You may be in a monogamous relationship, but if your partner engages in risky behavior the danger is great.

PHASES OF HIV INFECTION

HIV-positive

Antibodies are present in blood, but symptoms may not be exhibited. The virus can be transmitted even when no symptoms are present. Infected persons may not know they carry the virus.

Symptomatic (early)

Symptoms may include loss of appetite, weight loss, fever, night sweats, skin rashes, diarrhea, tiredness, lack of resistance to infection, or swollen lymph nodes. The term AIDS-related complex (ARC) is seldom used now. In the past it helped overwhelmed medical systems develop appropriate responses.

AIDS—Opportunistic infections

When the immune system is critically compromised, a variety of infections can take advantage of the "opportunity." Persons infected with HIV are not able to fight off the infections. As the symptoms appear, persons are sometimes said to have "full-blown AIDS" (T-cell count less than 200).

TESTING

Values of testing

Testing may assure early treatment.
It may also encourage responsible behavior.

Problems

Efforts to make testing mandatory raise questions about confidentiality and invasion of privacy.

Individuals may not want to assume the cost of testing. Insurance companies and governmental leaders have objected to the high cost of widespread testing.

Persons being tested need access to competent counseling.

6

A BURDEN TOO HEAVY

SUICIDE

The weight of this disease and the constellation of psychosocial stressors (such as guilt, low self-esteem, shame, alienation, fear, stigma, discrimination. . .) that surround it may drive the PWA (person living with AIDS) to consider taking his own life. On the physical level, the PWA is subject to debilitating weakness, wasting, constant fever, nagging diarrhea, the potential loss of mobility, the prospect of around-the-clock care, and vulnerability to any number of opportunistic diseases that can take his sense of touch, taste, sight, and mind. It is difficult to think of another disease that is so merciless and debilitating. It is no wonder that the thoughts of suicide are on the mind of everyone afflicted with this disease. The best suicide prevention might be giving the patient the space to vent feelings of despair to lessen the likelihood of unexpressed feeling welling up and overtaking him in a moment of crisis.

Etta Mae: Tim had signs of his illness for several months but we didn't make the connection. A rash had broken out all over his body and he had gone to doctor after doctor to try to get it cured. We learned later that it was one of those AIDS-related early symptoms. Tim probably was suspicious of the reason for the rash but was not willing to worry us without some proof.

At this stage in his life, Tim was living alone in an apartment. He and a young man named Bart had lived together for a length of time, being lovers and friends. Tim enjoyed Bart's keen mind and his ability to argue or discuss political and religious issues with

Tim. However, at some point their relationship Tim decided he needed his own space and he moved out into an apartment. His friendship with Bart continued, however, and Bart checked on Tim frequently to make sure he was doing all right. He loved Tim and made that clear to us and to Tim.

Fritz: In June of 1989, we were scheduled to make a trip to Mount Sequoyah, Arkansas, for a church conference. However, word came from Bart that Tim was in the hospital in Atlanta. He told us that Tim had tried to commit suicide the night before and was in the psychiatric ward at the hospital.

Etta Mae: Tim had made at least two different attempts to take his life in the same evening. Deeply depressed, he went out of the house after supper, stood in the middle of the street and contemplated throwing himself in front of an oncoming vehicle. Thankfully the cars stopped before hitting him.

Having failed to end his life in the street, he then went inside and decided to slash his wrists. Before doing that, though, he wrote a note and propped it on a chair right inside his door. It read, "Please handle my body with care and please wear gloves. I am HIV-positive." The note expressed his concern for other people's welfare, even in the midst of his own pain, even as he prepared to take his own life.

Fritz: The suicide attempts were not successful, but they did draw attention to the fact that Tim needed help with his HIV-positive status. He had a doctor's appointment the next day after the suicide attempt and mentioned to her what had happened the evening before. The doctor was immediately alarmed and had him admitted to the hospital that day. We needed help too. How could we support and encourage Tim in the most helpful way?

Etta Mae: We drew on our experience for guidance. A young girl in our local church had just attempted suicide, and her parents were not allowed to visit her. We assumed that might be standard procedure after a suicide attempt, so we did not offer to go to Atlanta, although that is where we wanted to be. We discovered later that the youth had *requested* that her parents not visit, and, after much discussion between Fritz and me, we decided that Tim would not make a similar request. So we got up our nerve to ask him if we could come to Atlanta to be with him. What a relief that was to him; he had been wanting to ask us but was afraid we didn't want to come. For some reason he still felt unsure of our love and how we would respond. We took the first available flight to be by his side.

Fritz: Our time together provided opportunity for clearing the air, "getting the house in order," making amends, experiencing some reconciliation. We uncovered some unresolved tensions in the parent-son relationship. Though it was painful work, this was a good time for Tim to name them, for us to reflect, and for all of us to let go of the hard times in our lives.

Etta Mae: The time to deal with adolescent conflicts is during adolescence, not after you are an adult and have carried those hurts in your hearts for many years.

At one point Tim told us how hard it was for him to grieve over what was happening to him and the losses he would suffer. He said, "If I could only cry, it would help a lot." When we asked why he couldn't cry, he said, "Because you have not given me permission to do that." We were stunned! We had thought that our sons had always been allowed to cry over anything they wanted to. Tim went on to say, "You two never cry. And if you don't cry, then I don't feel like I have the right to cry either." In the course of the conversation, we gave each other permission to cry, and many tears were shed during our stay with Tim. One instance was in our talking about the stance of The United Methodist Church in regard to homosexuality. I became very upset and began voicing my anger to and disappointment with my church. I became so irate I began to cry. I realized later that this gave Tim permission to do the same and to feel the same way.

Fritz: It became evident to us while we talked with Tim and his counselor that Tim suffered from severe depression, probably linked to the agony of living with a terminal illness. The doctor also suggested that he suffered from a lack of self-esteem. Maybe we knew this, but it seemed out of character for him. This was a young man who had remarkable gifts and abilities. Throughout his young life, he had registered an extraordinary list of accomplishments.

Etta Mae: He had been co-valedictorian of his high-school class of 500 students at Winnetonka High School in Kansas City; had been named Outstanding Math Student, Outstanding German Student, and Outstanding Male Vocalist.

Tim was also valedictorian of his college class at one of our United Methodist colleges—Central Methodist College in Fayette, Missouri. His degree was in music education. After graduating, he successfully taught elementary children in a small rural school in Faucett, Missouri.

Even though Tim enjoyed his two years of teaching, he sensed a call to ordained ministry. To test this call, he accepted a position as part-time youth worker at a large suburban Kansas City church. The experience confirmed his call, and he enrolled at Candler School of Theology in Atlanta to pursue a theological degree. Although he decided not to press so hard for academic grades, he still graduated cum laude.

Tim was a talented, intelligent, handsome young man. And yet, he didn't see himself that way. Surely his self-depreciation was linked to his struggle to accept himself as a gay man and to be accepted by The United Methodist Church that he loved. Did he feel God was against him, too? We don't know.

Fritz: During his tenure as public school teacher, before Tim came out to us, one of his elementary students began to label him "queer." The boy thought it was great fun, but the superintendent of schools did not. When the superintendent learned of the boy's campaign to slander Tim, he called the boy in and forced him to apologize to Tim. Afterwards Tim recounted the story to us, but he had not been ready at that time to come out of the closet in which he knew he was hiding.

Etta Mae: Ridicule was not a new experience. Belittlement of homosexual persons is one of the staples of our culture. It is no longer acceptable to target ethnic groups or to make jokes or sexual innuendos about women, but homosexuals are still fair game. The church of Jesus Christ—not just The United Methodist Church—often gives in to that same demeaning culture.

Fritz: While he was a student at Candler School of Theology, Tim joined the staff of a United Methodist church in the Atlanta area. He thoroughly enjoyed his work and consistently produced creative program ideas for children and youth. He had an excellent relationship with the senior pastor and the staff-parish relations committee. The members praised him for skill and leadership.

Then one day, Tim decided to participate in a gay rights rally in downtown Atlanta. It was, of course, the kind of event the media like to cover, for it dramatized conflict in society. On one side were confrontational advocates; on the other, equally confrontational opponents.

The television cameras captured Tim, and members of the church saw him on the evening news. While some members were supportive and said nothing was changed, a new senior pastor was now in leadership. He joined a large number of persons who pressed for Tim's resignation.

After an agonizing week, Tim submitted his resignation. The experience taught him that not only does The United Methodist Church consider homosexuality "incompatible with Christian teaching," some of its members also exhibit little tolerance for those who advocate for the human and civil rights of gay and lesbian persons.

Etta Mae: Incidents like these destroy one's self-worth. After a while one begins to believe, *I'm not worth anything if I'm incompatible with the Christian faith, incompatible with the teachings of the church I grew up in. Surely God and my family can't find much good in me.*

The church that had thought Tim was God's gift to them, many of whose members' children followed Tim like a Pied Piper, and many who thought Tim could do no wrong, within a day's time turned on him just because they assumed he was a gay man.

---

* Robert J. Perelli, *Ministry to Persons with AIDS: A Family Systems Approach* (Minneapolis: Augsburg, 1991), p. 26.

7

LEARNING TO LIVE WITH HIV/AIDS

I vividly recall a night in December or January about a year ago. It was 6:00 P.M., very cold, and getting dark. I was waiting for a bus to take me home, and I was standing behind a tree for protection from the wind. I had recently lost a friend to AIDS. From whatever measure of intuition God had given me, I knew suddenly and quite certainly that I also had AIDS. I stood behind the tree and cried. I was afraid. I was alone and I thought I had lost everything that was ever dear to me. In that place, it was very easy to imagine losing my home, my family, my friends, and my job. The possibility of dying under that tree, in the cold, utterly cut off from any human love seemed very real. I prayed through my tears. Over and over, I prayed: "let this cup pass." But I knew. Several months later, in April, a doctor told me what I had discovered for myself. Now it has been nearly a year. I am still here, still working, still living. I go to the doctor once a month and find myself reassuring him that I feel quite well. He mutters to himself and rereads the latest laboratory results which show my immune system declining toward zero.

Etta Mae: Tim came to Kansas City with us after about three weeks in the hospital. We had talked about numerous topics while he was hospitalized. At home we continued to work on emotional concerns.

AIDS is like a roller coaster. Tim's condition cycled through those ups and downs. He had no opportunistic diseases, but he was plagued with many of those irritating early symptoms: loss of appetite, skin rash, weariness, swollen lymph nodes.

43

During these days we set forth some tentative decisions. The first and most demanding task was for us to learn to live with AIDS. Tim's experience as a volunteer at AID Atlanta helped immensely. He had a long list of suggestions to strengthen our hope and to help him with the impending struggle.

Fritz: This was exactly what I needed in order to deal with my pessimism and resignation.

Etta Mae: It kept me realistic about the dreadful prognosis of HIV disease.

A problem emerged, however. After returning to Kansas City, we immediately took up our regular work schedule. Tim stayed at home all day by himself, except that I went home at lunch time to be with him. Because of our heavy work schedules, we spent much less time just sitting and talking. With hindsight far better than foresight, we concluded that it would have been much better had we stayed in Atlanta at Tim's home after he was released. The healing time would have been extended, and he would not have felt that he had been dumped in the middle of our lives with no place of his own.

Fritz: In due time, however, we made a decision that was important to us as we learned how to live with AIDS. We agreed that all of us would try to live our lives as normally as possible. I would keep my job. Etta Mae would keep her job. Tim would return to Atlanta and continue working as long as possible.

Etta Mae: Again, hindsight usually proves wiser. I regret not quitting my job and having the freedom to spend a week or more at a time with Tim and Fred. More emotional issues would have been resolved for all of us, I would have had the experience of taking care of them day by day, and I believe I would have felt that I had done a lot more for them and for myself.

Tim worked as a manager at a Kinko's store. He had taken a part-time job there after his forced resignation from the church where he worked during his seminary days. He expected to give up the Kinko's position when he graduated from seminary and he would be appointed somewhere. However, the General Conference of The United Methodist Church adopted legislation that forbade the ordination of "self-avowed, practicing homosexuals." Without dealing with any of the subtleties of this legislation,

Tim felt that the church had slammed the door in his face. His commitment to follow Christ's call into ministry was thwarted by the church he wanted to serve. He was considered "incompatible" and unwanted as a leader in the church. His bitterness (and mine) was never resolved.

Fritz: For several months, Tim continued to work at Kinko's. He even was promoted to a manager's responsibility. As time passed, however, he grew weaker and less able to handle the duties of a manager. Eventually he reduced his schedule to four days a week. This allowed him three days of recovery time and time for doctors' appointments.

---

[*] Terry Boyd, *Living with AIDS: One Christian's Struggle* (Lima, Ohio: C.S.S. Publishing Co., 1990), p. 31.

8

THE HARD TASK
OF TELLING OTHERS

Cars going first
one way, then another,
obscuring briefly my vision
of you.
Physical space delineated
by only my heart
reaches beyond.
I do not blink.
I cannot breathe.
I reach out to touch you—
but find only empty space.
But, I do see you—
if briefly obscured
by cars going first
one way, then another.*

Etta Mae: To this point we had told no one what our family was going through, feeling sure that repercussions would occur and we weren't ready to face them. It was hard enough dealing with the fact that two of our sons were seriously ill, without having to deal with the judgmental people who possibly would ostracize our sons or us. We had many good friends we could (and should) have told, but that fear was so strong—we just couldn't be sure how they might react. As we indicated earlier, many of our sons' friends had parents who would not accept their children because of their sexuality. If parents won't accept a lifestyle or an illness, how could we expect non-family members to be open and accepting?

Fritz: The summer of 1989 we joined very dear friends at Cedar

Crest Camp in Tennessee for the weekend. We had known John and Beth Gooch and Carl and Mary Lou Martin for almost thirty years. Our friendship with the Gooches goes back to our years at Central Methodist College. The four of us first came to know the Martins while we were students at Garrett-Evangelical Theological Seminary (GETS). The first Thanksgiving we were at GETS the six of us enjoyed the holiday dinner together. We continued to celebrate Thanksgiving together every year until our children became teenagers. They are dear people who have faced many hard issues themselves.

Etta Mae: Fifteen of us came together at Cedar Crest that summer. That included our seven children and two companions, one being Fred's lover, Rocky. It had been awhile since we had all been together so catching up was the first order on our agenda. We went around the room sharing what was going on in our lives, each one telling about his or her most recent experience. When it was time for Tim and Fred to share about their lives, they told of being ill with AIDS. How hard that was for them to share the fears they had, and for us, as their parents, to listen to them.

Fritz: Our friends enfolded our family in a blanket of love. What wonderful support they gave! What great care we received! These were friends we *knew* would not pull away from us or our sons, and they did not disappoint us.

Marty was with us for that weekend but was extremely quiet when it came time to share. His world was different from Tim's and Fred's since he was still in college and was wrapped up in college life. He was building relationships with his college friends and with the people in the town of Winfield, Kansas. He loved the town and wanted to settle there. His communication with Tim and Fred was infrequent and mostly through us. He saw them when they came home to visit, but did not pick up a phone to call them, nor did they call him. Marty had told only a couple of very close friends as he had heard too many jokes and comments regarding gays and didn't want to reveal that fact about his brothers. He purposely did not respond to acquaintances when comments were made as he was afraid his anger would get out of control. Thus it appeared that he didn't care, when deep inside he was hurting, sharing his deepest feelings with very few people.

Etta Mae: Besides our mothers, these were the only people we told. Our mothers were equally accepting, grieving along with us at the fate of Tim and Fred. One of the great gifts our mothers gave us and our sons was to greet them with a kiss on the mouth the first time they saw them after hearing of their illnesses! This was at a time when rumors flew wildly about how AIDS was contracted, but those grandmothers definitely showed their love for Tim and Fred. If we hadn't loved our mothers completely already, that would have cinched our love for them. Other people were afraid to come into the same room that Tim and Fred were in, but our mothers wrapped their arms around them and kissed them soundly. We are still awestruck with the realization of what happened.

Fritz: Not too long after revealing the news to our mothers, we told my sister and her husband, Sue and Larry Sonner. They provided wonderful family support and important counsel as well. Both work within the church, so their expertise was very helpful. Larry was then the Director of the Iowa Area Office of Pastoral Care, and offered us guidance out of his professional training also.

Etta Mae: I have a large extended family, but we were just not quite ready to share the bad news with them at this time. There was still that dread of how they would react.

---

* "One Way, Then Another" by Randall Poshek-Gladbach, a college classmate of Tim's.

9

FOUR MONTHS TO LIVE

Etta Mae: All three boys came home for Christmas in December 1989. We were so excited about having them, and I wanted to have everything just right for their arrival. However, I came down with a very severe case of the flu and was sick most of the week before their arrival. I was determined I would be well; and I literally dragged myself out of bed the day before in order to finish wrapping presents, cook their favorite food, and so on.

I was *not* over the flu. In fact, I was still contagious and Fred ended up with my germs. He became ill almost as soon as he returned to New York.

Fritz: During this illness, Fred constantly experienced the roller-coaster nature of AIDS. He tried to work but just couldn't keep up his energy level. When he worked full days, it became necessary for him to take every other day off. He cut his schedule to half-days and later to a half-day on the job followed by a whole day off. Finally, his supervisor suggested he take some sick leave and just stay home until he was over the flu. He gladly agreed to this. Eventually, he took temporary disability.

Etta Mae: We called him often to see how he was getting along, but we never had allowed ourselves to believe he was as sick as he really was. In early March I called to check on him and discovered he had not been out of bed for two weeks—not even to go to the bathroom or to eat meals. His companion of five years, Rocky, was providing a bedpan for Fred, and he was receiving hot meals through the Gay Men's Health Crisis.

I asked Fred if he had talked to the doctor, and he grunted that he had. I inquired what the doctor had said.

"The doctor told me I have the flu," he mumbled.

"No one has the flu for two months," I blurted out. "There must be something else wrong."

"Of course there is!" Fred shouted. "I have AIDS!"

"I know that," I replied, trying to be calm and helpful, "but I'm sure there is something the doctor can do to help during this illness."

I have great faith in doctors, and I just knew Fred's doctor could do something for him. There had to be a cure available. I told Fred I wanted him to go to the doctor right away or I was coming to New York and take him myself. A twenty-eight-year-old escorted to the doctor by his mother? Fred didn't think he wanted that to happen, so he got Rocky to take him to see the doctor. As I think back on that appointment, I cannot imagine how Fred walked to the subway, down to the train, and back up the steps to the doctor's office. We are grateful for the care Rocky provided, but I still feel badly just thinking how callous I was in not going and helping him get to the doctor, with transportation right from his door. Somehow he managed the steps, with Rocky's help, but how much simpler it would have been to have hired a cab. Money evidently was a bigger issue at that point than Fred's ability to walk.

Fritz: Rocky called us the next day and said he had bad news. The doctor had taken him aside and told him that Fred's condition had deteriorated drastically. He estimated that Fred had no more than two to four months to live. The doctor said he didn't think it was a good idea to tell Fred this as he thought Fred would just give up. It was March, and the doctor was telling us that our son might be dead by summer.

We suggested to Fred that perhaps he would like to come home for a visit, hoping he would just decide to stay with us. He did come, but he was restless all the time. He was ready to go back to New York—his home—within a week or so.

Etta Mae: Now, a major decision regarding disclosure had to be made. We could not let our son die with AIDS and not have any of

52

our friends know what was happening to him and to us. So it was time to test the compassion of our friends. It was time for us to let go of our fear and share this tragedy with others.

I began by sharing it with my employer, Dave Finestead, and my very dear friend Sue Ann Greer. I was not surprised by their responses. Both said, "Oh, no, not *both* of your sons!" Then they began to cry and continued to cry with me while we let out our grief. They enveloped me in their arms and into their hearts.

Fritz: Who else should we tell before the public was informed? We decided the place to start was with the colleagues with whom we worked. The first person for me to tell was my bishop, W. T. Handy, Jr. He had been a friend for many years. In 1980 he was elected to the episcopacy of The United Methodist Church and assigned to the Missouri Area. Through the years we became very close. Others saw him as professional, reserved, and rigid. I knew him as a caring colleague. In spite of our close relationship, I was not sure what response I would receive. I had never seen in his ministry any advocacy for gay and lesbian persons. Neither had I heard him support the official position of The United Methodist Church judging homosexual persons to be incompatible with Christian faith. How relieved I was when he responded with words of support and encouragement and an uncharacteristic hug. I was grateful for the prayer he offered that day.

At the time I was a district superintendent, serving with Bishop Handy in a supervisory capacity for The United Methodist Church in western Missouri. Etta Mae worked as a church secretary. My office was in the conference center, along with the offices of several others. After sharing with Bishop Handy, I sat down with my colleague district superintendent, Elroy Hines. Then I told our secretary. That same morning I invited all the persons working in the building to come together so that I might share the painful news. Each one responded with tears and hugs, with promises of prayer and pledges of support.

At the same time I shared with persons in the conference center, Etta Mae called her colleagues together and told them.

Etta Mae: I was still in staff meeting when a light tap came on the door. It was Steve Johnson, from Fritz's office. Their staff meeting was over and he came to talk to me. He said very little, and I can't remember exactly what it was. I do remember that he put his arms around me and said, "Fritz, just told us about your boys." He then went on to tell me how much he loved us and how he would do anything in the world to take away our hurt. We stood there and cried together. He went back to work. I went to the bathroom to reconstruct my teary face!

We had asked our staff people not to share this news with anyone as we just weren't ready for it to go public. However, within a couple of days, a clergy person called me to say he had heard about Tim and Fred; he wanted to express his deep concern for us. Instead of appreciating his call, I was furious! Who had leaked the news before we could do so ourselves? I lashed out at the caller and asked him where he had gotten this information. He, of course, said he couldn't remember where he had heard it and immediately apologized for calling. I'm sure he thought I was hell on wheels after that conversation, and I *think* I remember apologizing to him later for the way I acted. Grief does strange things to us. Anger is one of the reactions in the grief process.

Fritz: At about the same time we informed our colleagues, we decided it was just too painful and too draining to describe our plight over and over again.

Etta Mae: As I mentioned, I have a large extended family. We could not bear even to call each one of them personally. So we wrote a letter to my sister and three brothers. This was the time we also wrote to our "Christmas list" friends.

Right away the supportive responses poured in. We received telephone calls and letters by the hundreds. Many people notified us that we were included in their prayer list. One of those prayer groups remembering us was in a Baptist church in Florida and another in a Catholic church in Illinois. We never knew how our names reached their prayer circles. After the word got around, we ended up receiving more than seven hundred cards saying we were thought of and being prayed for.

Why did we ever doubt these dear people that we knew as our friends?

Fritz: One of the most touching responses came from Jay Krumeich and Holly Wood, our former associate pastors on the staff of First United Methodist Church in Blue Springs, Missouri.

They were living near St. Louis, about a six-hour drive from our home in Liberty, Missouri. After receiving our letter, Jay said to Holly, "Pack your bags. We are headed to Liberty to be with Fritz and Ett." Just about six hours later they arrived on our doorstep and rang the doorbell. Imagine the surprise and overwhelming gratitude we experienced when we opened the door and saw their wonderful faces. They simply said, "We got your letter and we have come to be with you." No more needed to be said; their presence indicated their love for us, and for Tim and Fred.

Etta Mae: April of 1990 came and went. May arrived and with it a phone call to Fred in which we discovered he was almost too weak to talk. When I asked him if he thought he should be in the hospital, he said yes, that would be a good idea. I suggested he call the doctor to arrange for him to be admitted to the hospital the next day, a Friday. I knew his friends were there with a car and could take him in. However, Fred said he didn't think he could ride in a car and needed an ambulance. My heart nearly stopped! If Fred were that sick, what would be the diagnosis once he got to the hospital? I was afraid to find out. Fritz and I got a flight out as soon as we could, flying from Kansas City to New York. It took most of the day by the time we arranged our schedules and flew into New York. Upon entering St. Vincent's Hospital, we found Fred still in the emergency room on one of those hard, cold gurneys.

Fritz: When we asked support staff why he wasn't in a room after spending ten to twelve hours in the emergency room, we were told there were no beds available on the AIDS ward. We knew there were two floors reserved for persons with AIDS at St. Vincent's. Was there no room on either unit? If not, why couldn't Fred be assigned to another floor so he could have a room and a comfortable bed? In a short time a bed was found on another unit, and Fred was taken there.

Etta Mae: As we adjusted to this room assignment, we discovered why the administration wanted to wait for a bed in the AIDS ward. The nurses on the other floors were not equipped for or trained to care for patients with AIDS. Their fear showed as they came in and out of the room. Everyone was happy when a bed became available and Fred was transferred to the appropriate ward.

Fritz: Fred's doctor was away for the weekend, and we missed his comforting spirit. The doctor on call was very competent, however. Because Fred's condition was critical, he asked us if we had considered a living will.

Etta Mae and I had talked about this for Fred, but he had never been included in the conversation. I believed strongly that a living will was an important thing to have. During years of pastoral ministry, I had visited hundreds of persons in intensive care units who were being kept alive by ventilators. Artificial life support seemed worse than death to me. I hoped that no one in our family would ever have to endure such humiliation. We are not bound by our fears of death. We believe that God always keeps us under providential care. Whether we live or die, we are still with the Lord. If there appears to be no hope for a meaningful life, then it seems best to let death bring its sweet release.

Etta Mae: Fred entered this discussion with less enthusiasm than we. He said, "Well, if there is hope that a life support system might help me recover, then I would want to have that chance." After a while, however, he was persuaded by our reasoning (and our pressure) and he signed the document. We also persuaded him to have a regular will drawn up, a service provided free of charge for him by the Gay Men's Health Crisis. We were grateful that a doctor had cared enough to broach the subject of a living will with us. In a different situation, we would hope that the pastor might have been the one to mention it. The social worker at the hospital was also helpful in making suggestions as to what we and Fred might want.

Fritz: Fred began to recover from his bout with pneumonia and by Sunday was doing fairly well—so well, in fact, that we decided to ask the doctor if he thought I could return to Missouri for the United Methodist Annual Conference. The physician observed that Fred was doing much better. He expected him to continue to improve to the point that he could return home within a few days. At the same time he reminded us of the terrible swings that accompany this illness. One day a patient is doing quite well; the next day he or she is perched on the threshold of death.

With that information in hand, we decided together that it would be all right for me to go home and attend the annual conference session. I flew out on a Sunday evening and drove to Fayette, Missouri, on Monday to attend the conference.

Etta Mae: I made the decision to stay in New York with Fred until he was well enough to go home. On Monday afternoon, Fred's condition began to worsen again. The nurses indicated, by their frantic actions, that Fred was not doing well and they even ushered me out of the room so they could get him stabilized. I was alone in New York with a very ill son, no support, not able to be in the room with Fred, and I was scared to death. Was I to be there alone when Fred died? Could I possibly handle this all by myself?

I was allowed back in the room after a short time, but it was clear to me that Fred might not make it through the night. Fritz called Monday evening from Fayette, and I shared what had been happening since he left.

Fritz: I could hardly talk to Etta Mae. Tears flooded my eyes, and guilt overwhelmed me. I was in the wrong place; I belonged in New York with Fred and Ett. It made matters worse when she indicated that Fred confided that he had really wanted me to stay.

Every decision has consequences. Many months ago we had decided to try to live our lives as normally as possible. On this occasion it was the wrong policy and the wrong decision. Unlike Etta Mae, who was in New York alone, I was surrounded by scores of my closest friends. The love and support I received from them was all that helped me make it through that morning. I knew that no matter what happened, my friends would be there with support.

Etta Mae: Fred didn't want me to leave that night, but St. Vincent's was extremely strict about visiting hours. He begged me to come earlier the next day (in other words, before visiting hours) and I inquired as to the possibity of doing so. No way, I was told. Visiting hours began at 1:00 P.M., you received a card from the information desk in order to visit, and you could not go through the doors without the card. So I went to Fred's apartment for the night, leaving a phone number where I could be reached in an emergency, and returned to visit him the next day. To my amazement, not only had he survived the night but he was looking much better!

Fritz: I was much relieved when I called the next day and found

Fred to be improving. God was at work in our lives, but AIDS is a terrible illness. The ebb and flow was wearing us out.

I stayed for the remainder of the week in Fayette, going back to New York when the conference was over.

Etta Mae: The church where I worked allowed me time off when I desperately needed it, so we were able to stay in New York with Fred for about two weeks. We still weren't sure if he would recover enough to go to his apartment. He was so weak. He could not stand up long enough even to be weighed, so the nurses tied a sheet around him and hung him up on scales to weigh him. He was around ninety pounds at this time and was five feet ten inches tall. He could not sit up for any length of time, could not walk from the bed to the chair in order to sit in it, and had to wear a catheter because he could not walk to the bathroom.

In this condition he announced to us one day that he was going to Alaska in July! It was now the second week in June.

Fritz: Our mouths dropped open and we exclaimed, "Alaska?" "Yes. Alaska in July." Impossible. The doctor had said Fred wouldn't even be here in July.

We suggested he might want to postpone that trip until later, when his strength had returned.

No, he already had the tickets bought.

Again, we suggested that he could get the tickets changed without too much trouble and we would even pay the extra fee for him.

No, he was going to Alaska in July!

Etta Mae: From the time he was little, he had been stubborn. This time we tried to overcome that stubbornness with sensibility. To no avail. Finally we said, "OK, he is twenty-eight years old and he is in charge of his own life." We dropped the matter and decided when it came closer to time we would talk to him again. We did ask his doctor if it would be possible for Fred to go, and he just shook his head. The nurses just chuckled when Fred told them he was going and made jokes with him about his mobility.

Fritz: The doctor took us aside one day and said, "I have done all that I can do for Fred. You might as well take him home."

We knew he was saying to us, "Take him home to die." So after a few days, we packed Fred up and we brought him back to Missouri. He wasn't really happy about that. Missouri wasn't his home; New York was his home. But we persuaded him it would be much easier to care for him at our home. Reluctantly, he agreed to come with us.

10

WENT TO ALASKA

In view of all this, what can we say? If God is for us, who can be against us? Certainly not God, who did not even keep back his own Son, but offered him for us all! He gave us his Son—will he not also freely give us all things? Who will accuse God's chosen people? God himself declares them not guilty! Who, then, will condemn them? Not Christ Jesus, who died, or rather, who was raised to life and is at the right side of God, pleading with him for us! Who, then, can separate us from the love of Christ? Can trouble do it, or hardship or persecution or hunger or poverty or danger or death? As the Scripture says,
"For your sake we are in danger of death at all times;
    we are treated like sheep that are going to be slaughtered."
No, in all these things we have complete victory through him who loved us! For I am certain that nothing can separate us from his love: neither death nor life, neither angels nor other heavenly rulers or powers, neither the present nor the future, neither the world above nor the world below—there is nothing in all creation that will ever be able to separate us from the love of God which is ours through Christ Jesus our Lord.
                                                   —Romans 8:31-39

Etta Mae: Fred was with us for two-and-a-half weeks when he said, "I need to get back to New York now. It is about time for my trip to Alaska."

Fritz: By this time he was walking around the house with a cane, but he was not going any great distances. We took him shopping

61

for some clothes that would fit him, and we put him in a wheelchair so he wouldn't have to walk far.

Once again we said, "Fred, we don't think you are well enough to go to Alaska. Let's reconsider this trip."

"No," he said, just as firmly as before. "I want to go back to New York."

So we took him to the airport. He managed to walk onto the plane himself, using his cane. We wondered how he would survive walking around Alaska with a cane! We rejoiced with him that he was able to make the trip, but at the same time we thought, "This is going to be the last time we see Fred alive."

Etta Mae: He went to Alaska with Rocky as his guide and driver. We asked him to please call us at least once from Alaska while he was there. Sure, he would do that. And he did. He called twice, in fact. The first call was just a day or so after he arrived, and he simply wanted us to know that he had made the trip all night. He had suffered some on the plane trip from too much sitting with very little padding. He also had a problem with his legs aching but reported that he just took some aspirin and gritted his teeth!

His second call came at the end of the first week. Fred said, "This is the most wonderful place on earth." He described beautiful mountains rising from the ocean, amazing glaciers, a herd of mountain sheep, and a bear with her two cubs.

He told us about the day he had just experienced. They drove to a ghost town, he said. The abandoned community happened to be across the river at the end of a gravel road down which they had driven. In order to get to the ghost town, tourists had to ride in a small tram operated by a pulley system.

Fritz: We said, "How in the world did you operate it? You don't have any strength in your arms." He told us there were two other people in the lift with him who actually did the pulling. He also said there were park rangers on either side of the river who helped him. Unfortunately, one man on the car was extremely heavy, and his weight made the tram tilt. That wouldn't have been so bad if there had been a gate to close to keep them securely inside, but the tram was open on one side. The guide had told them if they fell out of the car and into the icy river they would surely be in danger of dying from hypothermia. Fred said, "I wasn't pulling to move the lift, I was hanging on for dear life just to stay in!"

Etta Mae: We asked what happened after they got safely across. "Was the ghost town right there on the river bank?" "Oh, no," he said, "it was about a half a mile away." We asked him how they got there, thinking perhaps there was another bus to transport them. Fred replied nonchalantly, "We walked." Even over the telephone he must have heard our mouths drop open. He walked. He walked for one half of a mile and another half of a mile back to the river. How did he do that? This man, who could only walk a short distance with a cane when he left Missouri, walked a mile. We realized that some sort of a miracle had taken place while he was in Alaska.

Fritz: While Fred was in Alaska, his doctor in New York called us in Kansas City and said he was worried about Fred. He had tried to call him several times at his apartment and couldn't reach anyone. He was concerned that something had happened to him. We said, "Oh, no, he's fine. He's in Alaska." There was complete silence on the other end of the phone. He was even more stunned than we were that Fred had made the trip.

Etta Mae: We received another call that week. It was from Belinda Jo Williams, a college friend of Fred's. She indicated that she had talked with him before he left for Alaska. She was concerned that he was not being honest when he told her he was doing better.

During the conversation, Jo made an entirely unexpected disclosure: Fred was a father! Siobhan Marie, then seven years old, had been born on January 27, 1983, after a short, intimate relationship between Jo and Fred when they were students at Columbia College in Columbia, Missouri.

Fritz: We were shocked, since Fred had never given us any indication of this episode in his life. We spent a long time trying to absorb this new information and adjust to its meaning for our present and future. Fred had only seen the child when she was a baby. He apparently had assumed no responsibility for Siobhan's support, nor had Jo asked for it. We prayed for grace and wisdom to handle this new reality.

In the intervening years, we have come to know Siobhan. We

have welcomed her into our family and been delighted to have her visit. As Siobhan has matured we have taken pride in her talent as a musician and a dramatist, her achievement as a scholar and her skill as a writer. We enjoy telling people how beautiful our grand-daughter is.

Etta Mae: Fred and Rocky came back through the Kansas City area on their way home since Fred wanted to attend his tenth high school reunion. We eagerly awaited their arrival at the airport, expecting that he would be wheeled from the airplane to the ter-minal. As we watched, here he came, walking up the jetway as though he had never been sick. He looked healthy and happy, hav-ing put on several pounds since we had last seen him. The appetite pills the doctor had prescribed in order to encourage him to eat more were a success. Rocky said they had to stop at every conven-ience store, every grocery store, every restaurant they passed in order to get food for Fred. He ate his way through Alaska! It was hard to fill him up. But he filled up and out and looked good.

Fritz: Alaska is one of those wonderful symbols for us. It became our sign of hope. When we talked about the Alaska trip we started to believe that AIDS could be whipped. Fred could get well.

This symbol expanded our entire outlook on life. If suffering and pain were to be our lot, the journey would not be in vain. There is a larger context that affirms the words in scripture: "If God is for us, who is against us" (Romans 8:31 NRSV).

Etta Mae: When we created the Names Project Quilt panel months later, we included a symbol for Alaska.

When you are living with AIDS, you have to have something to hope for. The Christian faith is our bedrock. We believe in resur-rection. We believe that even though we die, yet shall we live by faith in Jesus Christ. We believed this even as our sons suffered. We believe it even more firmly because of what we have been through.

Fritz: By nature we do not carry a burden of anger around with us. Elisabeth Kübler-Ross identifies anger as one of the emotional responses to expect in time of grief. We never got stuck on anger. We simply trusted God to see us through this ordeal. As we con-tinue the journey, the healing Spirit and the living Christ will be with us.

11

DANCING IN A WHEELCHAIR

Fritz: Fred never talked about dying. We sometimes felt that he never thought he would. Even so, it seemed to us that Fred tried to accomplish three closure tasks that summer. One, he wanted to go to Alaska; two, he wanted to go to his friend's wedding; and three he wanted to go to his high school class's tenth reunion.

Etta Mae: Jo Holman's wedding took place prior to the Alaska trip. In fact, the marriage celebration occurred in June, the day after we brought Fred from New York to our home in Liberty. At that time he couldn't even stand or walk. He was completely dependent on a wheelchair. In spite of his limitations, friends picked him up and took him to the early afternoon wedding. After the ceremony, he went to his friends' apartment and stayed there all afternoon. In the evening they all attended the wedding reception.

We worried about him and kept wishing he would call to say he wanted to come home. We knew his energy level was low and he needed rest. But he did not call before the time we had scheduled for us to pick him up from the reception. When we arrived, he was having a great time with his friends, visiting and *eating*. He was not ready to go home yet.

Fritz: As we watched the festivity, just as the band was ready to strike up another number, Jo, the bride, came to Fred and invited him to dance. She held his hand as he wheeled onto the dance floor. Together they danced to her happiness and their friendship.

Fred danced in a wheelchair! In all our experience with suffering and pain, we know of no more powerful symbol of hope than dancing in a wheelchair.

Etta Mae: The third closure activity was his high school class reunion. He took Rocky with him, having fun introducing him to all his friends, which we thought was very courageous of him. Once again, his courage and grit came through. He was determined to be the person God created him to be, and he wanted to show this to the world.

Even though he looked healthy to us (after being near death), he surely must have looked emaciated to his classmates. That was not a concern of his, however; he simply wanted to renew friendships. We never talked with any of his classmates who hadn't known about his illness, so we cannot know how they actually responded to him at their reunion. According to Fred's report, everyone was congenial, so he evidently felt no hostility, animosity, or pity from any of them.

12

TRAPPED BY AIDS

The LORD says,
"My servant will succeed in his task;
 he will be highly honored.
Many people were shocked when they saw him;
 he was so disfigured that he hardly looked human.
But now many nations will marvel at him,
 and kings will be speechless with amazement.

They will see and understand
 something they had never known."

The people reply,
"Who would have believed what we now report?
 Who could have seen the LORD's hand in this?
It was the will of the Lord that his servant
 grow like a plant taking root in dry ground.
He had no dignity or beauty
 to make us take notice of him . . .
 nothing that would draw us to him.
We despised him and rejected him:
 he endured suffering and pain.
No one would even look at him—
 we ignored him as if he were nothing."
                                    —Isaiah 52:13–53:3

Fritz: That summer, our family enjoyed some time together at our home in Liberty. Fred, as we noted earlier, came home with us from New York, and Tim came from Atlanta to spend three days. Marty was not able to join the family at that time. We regretted his absence because it was difficult for the rest of us in the family to know how he was coping with this struggle.

When we picked Tim up from the airport, he looked gaunt and tired. He was not able to keep up with our normal pace of walking and asked that we slow down to walk with him.

Etta Mae: We could see that Tim's condition had deteriorated considerably. Since the test that confirmed his HIV-positive status, he had remained fairly stable. The skin rashes continued without much relief. He also experienced increasing difficulty with thrush, a disease caused by a fungus which is marked by white patches and coating in the mouth. He also had to endure neuropathy, which causes a numbness of the feet. (Fred had complained of this for some time, also.) The most serious problem was the precipitous erosion of his T-cell count.

CELL-MEDIATED IMMUNITY

Cell-mediated (cellbound) immunity is controlled by lymphocytes and provides resistance against viruses, fungi, protozoa, and mycobacteria (tuberculosis-like organisms). AIDS specifically damages this part of the immune system by altering the characteristics, numbers, and functions of the lymphocytes. T-lymphocytes are the central actors in this system and are the most seriously affected by AIDS.

There are three types of T-lymphocytes: (1) T-helpers (Th) which stimulate an immune response; (2) T-suppressers (Ts) which limit or inhibit immune response, and (3) T-killers (Tk) which directly destroy foreign invaders or antigens. T-killers are especially important in the destruction of fungi, protozoa, viruses, and certain cancers. . . .

Under normal circumstances the presence of antigens provokes an immune response. In AIDS, however, the total numbers of lymphocytes is depleted; but more specifically, there is a dominant number of T-suppressors due to a reduction of the T-helpers. Because T-suppressors dominate or prevent immune responses to fungi, protozoa, and viruses, opportunistic infections occur.[*]

Fritz: Tim was still working full time at Kinko's, with the four-days-on and three-days-off plan. It was a good place for him to be, for he received encouragement and support from his employer and the health benefits were excellent. Even so, he felt trapped there. He knew that he would have to maintain his employment there the rest of his life. If he resigned, it would be nearly impossible for him to secure medical insurance coverage on his own or in another position. This was a most important issue at a time when he knew frequent hospitalizations were inevitable and prescription costs were beyond reach without insurance.

The average cost for each hospitalization Tim and Fred endured was between $15,000 and $25,000. It is easy to see why we were so grateful for the enlightened policies at Kinko's (Tim's employer) and at Banker's Trust (Fred's employer). It seems quite ironic that the businesses that employed Tim and Fred were quite willing to have them there, whereas the church had basically thrown Tim out. Just where do we find Christianity?

Persons living with AIDS may need guidance regarding medical insurance. This is a service congregations can provide. In the earlier years of the pandemic, employers fired workers they discovered had AIDS. Neither employers nor insurance companies wanted catastrophic costs added to their annual claims payments. Now, federal law requires the insurer to provide for the availability of continued health insurance coverage in the event of a termination. Of course, the individual will be required to pay the premium. If one does not have a job, it is impossible to raise enough money to pay premiums. Many companies now provide for continuation of coverage, but when you are relating to people in your community, you need to help them ask that question: How are you going to provide for health insurance and hospitalization care?

An AIDS Support Team in a congregation could gather information and have it readily available for persons when the information is needed. The Team could also solicit contributions to an emergency assistance fund. Grants could be made to offset some medical costs not covered by insurance.

Etta Mae: Tim was aware of his declining condition as we were. One evening as we talked with him over the phone, he announced, "This has been the worst day of my life. I tried to give my body away, but nobody will take it. All the recipient agencies are afraid of an HIV-infected body. I have tried several places, but none is interested in having my body after I die."

We laughed, but there were tears mixed with our laughter.

---

* From *Living With AIDS: A Self-Care Manual,* edited by Jennifer M. Lang, Judith Spiegel, and Stephen M. Strigle, and published by AIDS Project Los Angeles, Inc., 1986, pp. 11-12.

13

TWO HOSPITALIZATIONS AT THE SAME TIME

From inside the fish, Jonah prayed to the LORD his God:
When I was in trouble, LORD, I prayed to you,
   and you listened to me.
From deep in the world of the dead,
   I begged for your help, and you answered my prayer.

You threw me down to the bottom of the sea.
The water was churning all around;
   I was completely covered by your mighty waves.
I thought I was swept away from your sight,
   never again to see your holy temple.

I was almost drowned by the swirling waters that sur-
rounded me.
Seaweed had wrapped around my head.
I had sunk down below the underwater mountains.
   I knew that forever, I would be a prisoner there.

But, you, LORD God, rescued me from that pit.
When my life was slipping away, I remembered you—
   and in your holy temple you heard my prayer.

All who worship worthless idols turn from the God who
offers them mercy.
But with shouts of praise, I will offer a sacrifice to you,
my LORD.
I will keep my promise, because you are the one with
power to save.

                                          —Jonah 2:1-9 CEV

71

Fritz: In October 1990, Fred called to report: "I am back in the hospital. This time I have CMV." Cytomegalovirus is another of the opportunistic infections associated with AIDS. It may occur without any symptoms or result in mild flu-like symptoms such as aching, fever, or sore throat. Severe CMV can lead to hepatitis, mononucleosis, or pneumonia. Obviously Fred's case was serious enough to warrant hospitalization. At this point the infection had led to the loss of sight in one of Fred's eyes.

The doctor urged Fred to enter the hospital for treatment in order to guard against the risk of blindness in the other eye. He needed to be in the hospital so the medication could be administered intravenously. We called him daily and were reassured each time that he was doing well.

Fred had received treatment for about a week. Then the doctor told him he could teach him how to medicate himself at home. "We'll put in a shunt," he said, "and you will be able to give the medication to yourself." Fred was delighted with that proposal, as he hated being in the hospital. The surgical procedure to implant the shunt was completed, and Fred prepared to go home.

Etta Mae: Tim called us from Atlanta the same day Fred was to be released. He told us he was back in the hospital with pancreatitis. This is still another of the several opportunistic infections we now encountered with regularity. This inflammation of the pancreas causes extreme nausea. Tim could not eat or drink anything. He couldn't even munch on ice chips, since everything that went into his mouth came right back up. So he was in the hospital being fed intravenously. I asked if he needed some moral and physical support and he jumped at the chance to have his mother come down. I flew to Atlanta the next day.

Fritz: I flew to New York for a meeting of the General Board of Global Ministries the same day that Etta Mae flew to Atlanta. I had planned to check into the hotel after arrival, spend the night, and then go to Brooklyn the next morning to see Fred.

When I arrived at the hotel there was an emergency message at the desk. The note from Rocky read: "Fred is in the intensive care unit at the hospital."

Etta Mae: Fritz's phone call came to me in Tim's room at Crawford Long Hospital, saying he was headed for St. Vincent's.

All the information he had was what was in the note, so we were both left wondering what had happened. There was nothing to do but wait until he had more information, so I paced the floor in the hospital room, occasionally grabbing Tim's outstretched hand for support. Once again, Fritz and I were separated at a time when we needed each other's strength. As Tim and I talked about what was happening to both him and Fred, Tim said, "Mom, don't you wish sometimes that we would both just die and get it over with?" Oh, Tim, never would I wish that, because I love you both so much. That question from Tim stabbed at my heart, making me wonder if that was what Tim was wishing himself. As for me, I wanted to hang on to them as long as possible, but I didn't want them to suffer.

Fritz: St. Vincent's Hospital was only a short distance away from the hotel, so, even though it was late, I hopped on the subway and went to the hospital to see what had happened. Just as the note indicated, I found Fred in the intensive care unit—and he was on a respirator!

"Why is he on a respirator?" I demanded of the staff in an angry voice. "Did you know that Fred has a living will, which forbids attaching him to the machine?" The nurse responded patiently, "Fred gave permission in order to save his life." I admitted to myself that probably he did give that directive.

His order forced us to rethink our position against the use of respirators, and we have backed away somewhat from our adamant stance against life support. Fred would never have survived this episode had he not had the ventilator at that time. Still, we have very strong feelings that artificial life support undermines the quality of living.

The next morning I went to the hospital early. I was sitting outside the intensive care unit in the hallway when Fred's doctor got off the elevator down the hall. As he came closer, he recognized me. He walked up, shaking his head, and said, "Went to Alaska."

"Yes, sir!" I answered. "Fred went to Alaska. Isn't he amazing?"

Etta Mae: All the medical personnel cared deeply for our sons. We found that the doctors (and the nurses) became very involved with the HIV/AIDS patients. Perhaps it was because they got to know them so well during those frequent hospital stays. Tim and

Fred received the care they needed and wanted, but who was taking care of Fritz and me? How could we ever have made it without God's sustaining presence? How could we have endured without the endless prayers of persons in so many places?

Fritz: What had happened to Fred this time? Why was he in the hospital again? The doctor related that Fred had been scheduled for release the day before. However, infection developed around the catheter in his chest, as had happened on two other occasions. This time the inflection lapsed into septic shock, with his temperature reaching 107 degrees, and he had to be taken to the intensive care unit. I asked about the prognosis, and the doctor said we would have to wait and see.

It was not long until Fred began to rally. One more time he mustered his will to live and fought back from the brink of death. Once more the AIDS roller coaster made its terrifying run.

As he gained strength, the doctor suggested they leave the shunt out and suspend the anti-CMV medication. Following this suggestion, he acknowledged, incurred the risk that Fred would lose his vision in the remaining, sighted eye. Fred's response was, "I would rather be dead than be blind. Put the shunt back in." Another Hickman catheter was implanted, and Fred soon improved enough to return home.

Etta Mae: While Fred was in intensive care, of course there was no way for me to talk to him. All the information I received came through Fritz, which was dependable, but I wanted to hear Fred's voice. The day he was released from ICU, he called me at home. He voiced exactly what I had been thinking. He said, "Mom, I know you wanted to hear from me directly, and I could hardly wait to get out so I could call you and tell you I love you." Oh, Fred, how I loved you, too. What a relief it was to know that he was recovering and to hear his strong voice.

Fritz: The day Fred was able to go back to a room, he showed his improvement to us by spending a couple of hours in the waiting room, playing cards with his friends. He had been confined to bed too long, and he wanted no more of that.

Etta Mae: The doctors who treated Tim and Fred were quite different in their approach to the illness. Fred's doctor let Fred take the lead on what he wanted or didn't want, depending mostly on how Fred felt while on certain drugs. Tim's doctor, on the other hand, was much more aggressive. She wanted Tim to try every experimental drug that was available, and Tim agreed to this. The doctor who treated Tim was known nationally for her AIDS expertise and spent much of her time traveling to conferences or to speaking engagements. Tim was willing to be one of her "guinea pigs," not only to try for some success against his own ailments but also to be able to help others who might contract this disease in the future. Tim's doctor treated him as was fitting for Tim's personality, and the same was true of Fred's doctor. We have the deepest appreciation for both of them and for their different styles.

14

"I'M READY TO DIE"

God is our shelter and strength,
   always ready to help in times of trouble.
So we will not be afraid, even if the earth is shaken
   and mountains fall into the ocean depths;
even if the seas roar and rage,
   and the hills are shaken by the violence.
                                          —*Psalm 46:1-3*

Etta Mae: In late October Tim entered the hospital with the suspicion that he had pneumonia. However, his penis and gums were bleeding, an indication that something else was wrong. He received a blood transfusion immediately, and the doctor ran a gallein scan in order to better see Tim's lungs. It revealed what we had feared—Kaposi's sarcoma in the lungs. That dreaded cancer had arrived. It could be treated with chemotherapy, but only after the pancreatitis had been cleared up.

In its classic form, Kaposi's sarcoma arises primarily on the lower legs of elderly males and follows a relatively limited and painless course. In connection with AIDS, it is much more aggressive and is not confined to older men. The tumors may occur anywhere on the body and frequently involve internal organs at a fairly early stage in its development. To observers, blotches on the face are the telltale signs that KS has emerged. Fearful viewers quickly stigmatized those who exhibited the signs. Tim was aware that he had KS on his penis. He experienced considerable pain with it, for it would scab over and make it impossible to urinate. A catheter had to be inserted in order to empty the bladder, but the catheter itself caused great pain. We learned later that Tim had Kaposi's sarcoma all through his body. We suspect that he never knew this.

Fritz: At Thanksgiving time (1990) we went to visit Tim in Atlanta. He had been in and out of the hospital, and when we arrived we found him back in the hospital receiving a blood transfusion. He had several transfusions during the course of his illness. Tim was very ill at this time. Although he had gone in for a blood transfusion, many other symptoms had appeared. He now had thrush, diarrhea to the point of wearing diapers all the time, pancreatitis, hepatitis, and tuberculosis. All of these plagued him at the same time.

Tim had wanted to entertain us for Thanksgiving. He was so unhappy that he was not able to fix us Thanksgiving dinner at his home, but we assured him we didn't mind that; being with him was the important thing.

Etta Mae: We stayed with Tim through the Thanksgiving weekend. Because he was ill I wanted to stay in his room at nights. Fritz slept at Tim and Bart's house.

Late in the evening of the night before we were to go back to Missouri, Tim began hyperventilating. Fritz had already gone back to Tim's house, so I was there by myself with Tim. Tim had mentioned to us that he was tired of the fight to live and wondered when it would be over. As he lay in bed, gasping for breath, he indicated that he didn't want heroic measures taken. I wasn't sure what was going on, as I had never seen anyone hyperventilate. I rang for the nurses and they just made light of it. One even said, "Oh, Tim, you know you always do this when you are in here." I certainly didn't know that had happened before. I simply wanted them to do something to ease his breathing. They just went about their business as usual, being very calm in handling him. Perhaps that was the best way to stabilize him, but at the time I wanted faster results and paced back and forth, trying desperately to think of something I could do myself.

That same night Tim awakened me about midnight and said, "I need to talk." Of course I was ready to respond to his request. So I got up from the cot and we talked and talked and talked, about everything imaginable. Then, without any warning that it was coming, Tim said, "I'm ready to die now. And I want to do this while you and Dad are here in Atlanta."

Tim had a brilliant mind and always had control of his life. As we described earlier, he could do almost anything he set out to do and do it well, and this was something he believed he could do—will himself to die.

The bluntness of the statement took me by surprise, but then reality hit me. I was overwhelmed by the implications of his wish. Tears choked my response. We decided to call Fritz and ask him to come to the hospital. At that point I was crying so profusely that Tim himself had to make the call to his dad.

Fritz: Tim's call came about 2:00 A.M. Bart took the call and woke me. As quickly as we could, the two of us dressed and drove to the hospital.

The parking garage was closed, so we parked the car in a lot across the street from the hospital. As we crossed Peachtree Street, a car full of young men roared by. "Fags!" they screamed at us. In the midst of our present crisis the ever present hatred against homosexual persons rose again. As I crossed the street I got a tiny taste of what it is like to try to live in this hostile culture. I knew a bit of the fear that gay persons bear every day.

Tim's account of the night he was mugged in Charleston came to mind. On a vacation trip, he was walking to his hotel one night when three thugs came up behind him, pushed him down, and hit him in the head with a brick. "That's what you deserve, you fag," they sneered. The memory of that report from Tim plus the present incident made me admire and love Tim even more for all he had gone through just being who he was.

Etta Mae: After Fritz and Bart reached Tim's room, the four of us sat around the bed and talked. Tim told us again what he wanted that night. After an hour or so, Tim sighed, "I guess my mind is willing, but my body isn't ready." He was right. Death stayed away that night. In just a few hours he began to get somewhat better.

The doctor said Tim could go home on Monday, if we could arrange for home nursing care. With the help of the social worker, we contacted an agency and planned for around-the-clock care. With him safely home and well cared for, we headed back to Kansas City.

Tim assured us he would come home for Christmas, even knowing how hard it would be. We were looking forward to this time when the whole family would be together again.

About three weeks later, one week before Christmas, in 1990, Tim called and said he could not make the trip. We were terribly disappointed. "We really want you to come," we said. "Why do you think you can't come?"

"First of all, I have to have a hospital bed." We assured him we had already checked that out and knew right where to rent one. He then said, "I have to have a wheelchair." I told him there was one at the church where I worked and we would bring it home. Then Tim said, "I need nurses to give me my medication." We had already contacted some nurses who were standing by, ready to take care of Tim when he came home. Then Tim said, "I can't come home. I am hooked up to IVs. I can't take that pole on the airplane, and I certainly can't drive." At this point we conceded that it would be impossible.

We decided we would go to Atlanta, along with Fred and Marty. We would all celebrate Christmas together at his place. That sounded good to Tim. However, I couldn't quite believe he was as sick as he told us. I was definitely in denial about his condition and pretended to myself that he could make it if he really wanted to. I *was* aware of all his ailments, but the mother in me said my son would be all right—and I claim to be an intelligent person!

15

"I'M DYING"

O God, you've allowed death to take him away,
leaving me alone
in the chill dawn of unfinished love.
What could you have been thinking?

Ungiven gifts pile about me.
Unsung songs remain
trapped in my throat.
Unsaid words lie rotting
in my mouth,
and I sit staring down
a lifetime of unlived days,
for love didn't leave
when death arrived.

God, what will I do
with the unfinished love?
It wells up within me
with nowhere to go,
and I am bursting
with the pain of it.

Come to me, O Comforter,
come to me.
Hold me against the pain
for just awhile
so that I might catch my breath.
Come to me, O Comforter,
and give me peace.

O God, I don't understand all this.
Give me your peace

that passes understanding.
Give me the grace
that only you can give,
the grace that overflows with peace,
so that I might spend my days
telling all who would hear
that you, O God—
*you are the answer**

Etta Mae: We called Tim every day after that. When we called on Thursday night (five days before Christmas) he was gasping for breath.

"What's going on, Tim?" we asked anxiously. "You sound like you are having a terrible time breathing. Why can't you breathe?"

"I'm dying," he answered with a voice so weak we could hardly hear him.

"Just hang on. We're going to be there on Saturday," I said, trying to put a positive note in the conversation.

"I don't know if I can make it that long," Tim whispered.

Fritz: We were aghast. We knew this was serious so we talked to his nurse to try to gain some perspective and understanding. Maybe that would offset our fears. She said Tim had requested her to remove all medications. He even wanted the painkillers turned off. She indicated that he had made that decision himself. She reminded us that she was required to follow his directions. She assured us that death doesn't come immediately after that, so she thought we could go ahead and keep our Saturday flight schedule.

The next day, Friday, the nurse called about 7:00 A.M. and urged, "You'd better get on a plane as quickly as you can. Tim is not doing well." As soon as we hung up the phone we began efforts to purchase plane tickets. Our efforts were not fast enough. While we were still making arrangements, the nurse called back.

"Tim has died," she told us.

It was December 21, 1990. Tim was thirty years old. Neither of us said much. We just held each other and cried. This battle with AIDS was lost. We knew we had to face another one sometime, but we did not know when.

Many misgivings poured out of our souls. Why didn't we go

yesterday? Why did Tim choose to take himself off medication when he did, knowing we would be there soon? Had he changed his mind, and no longer wanted us to be present when he died? Had he willed himself to die, just as he had wanted to do at Thanksgiving time?

Etta Mae: We later learned from his nurse that when she arrived on Friday morning to take care of him, she realized how short his time was. She made the decision then to hook him back up to medication and feedings, in order to keep him alive long enough for us to get to Atlanta. She said she knew that if it were she lying there, her parents would want to see her one more time. After she left the room to get the equipment, Tim died. We think he knew that the nurse was planning to restore his medications and was determined not to let that happen. The nurse also told us if she had done as planned and if someone had reported her, she would probably have lost her license to practice. She was willing to take that risk in order for two parents to see their dying son one more time.

Again our earlier decision came back to haunt us. We wanted to be there when death came, but we had chosen to live our lives where our work was. When you make decisions, you have to live with them. You can't always be where you'd like to be when you make decisions like that. We had let the nurse convince us that Tim would live until we arrived two days later, because we *wanted* to believe that.

Would I do the same thing again? I don't think so. I realize now, as the members of his cabinet told Fritz, "Nothing is normal." So why did we think we could maintain a normal life with death lurking in every corner? We should have gotten on a plane as soon as we heard Tim struggling to breathe. Our jobs weren't very important after all; taking care of and loving our sons was the important issue.

* Ann Weems, *Psalms of Lament* (Louisville: Westminster John Knox Press, 1995), pp. 12-13.

16

CELEBRATING DEATH AND RESURRECTION

Our help is in the name of the LORD
who made heaven and earth.
                                        —*Psalm 124:8 NRSV*

Listen, I will tell you a mystery! We will not all die, but
we will all be changed. . . . For this perishable body must
put on imperishability, and this mortal body must put on
immortality. . . . Then the saying that is written will be
fulfilled:
       "Death has been swallowed up in victory."
"Where, O death, is your victory?
Where, O Death, is your sting?" . . .
But thanks be to God, who gives us the victory through
our Lord Jesus Christ.
                              —*1 Corinthians 15:51-56 NRSV*

Etta Mae: Phone calls went out to Marty and Fred to tell them of the death of their older brother, Tim. We made those phone calls ourselves, grieving over the phone with them. Fred had Rocky present to help him absorb his grief, but Marty was at the radio station where he worked, and his co-workers hardly seemed aware of what was happening. He had no alternative but to go to his home and grieve in private.

Fritz: The Services of Death and Resurrection are meant to celebrate the life of the deceased. They do so in the context of worship and praise, prayers for comfort, and words of hope in witness to the living Christ.

Etta Mae: Since Tim had lived in Atlanta for some time, we

wanted to have a service with his friends there. After his resignation from the staff of his church, he had not been actively involved
in a congregation. In consultation with Bart, we decided to have a
memorial service at his home. This setting offered an intimate
space where friends could remember and give thanks.

Fritz: Tim had directed that his body be cremated. His friend,
Bart, made arrangements for a funeral home to care for this task.
At the time, it was not uncommon for mortuaries to refuse to handle the body of someone who had been infected with HIV. In this
case, the staff was courteous and helpful.

We called a pastor friend from one of the Atlanta churches and
invited him to preside. The service was held on Saturday, the day
after Tim's death. We were pleased and amazed that many of Tim's
seminary classmates came, as well as his "buddy." He had
acquired this buddy as a service from AID Atlanta—a person who
came periodically to see that Tim's needs were met. He had been
acquainted with her about a month. We were delighted that his
nurse and one of his doctors also attended. As we sat in a circle in
the living room, each one shared a recollection or a word of trib-
ute. It was a moving experience.

Etta Mae: One of Tim's classmates from seminary sobbed
throughout the entire service. Finally, at the close, she came to me
and put her arms around me. She then revealed the reason for her
tears: "I don't even deserve to be here today. I did not take good
care of or tend to Tim when he was alive; therefore, I have no right
to be here to honor him." We assured her we were glad she had
come, but I'm sure that guilt will stay with her a long time.

Our flight plans needed to be changed again since there was no
need for Fred and Marty to go to Atlanta for Christmas. We were
now planning a funeral rather than celebrating Christ's birth. We
had contacted a friend to meet Fred at the airport since we would
not be back in Liberty by the time he arrived. Marty was driving
home from Winfield, Kansas, and was to arrive before we got home.

Marty still wasn't in Liberty when we got back from Atlanta. He
had left a message at our home that his car had broken down about
an hour out of Winfield. That had been several hours before, and
no other word had come from him. We had no idea where he was
and tried to contact him through friends, but to no avail.

Finally, in early evening he contacted us to say he was on his way. He had left his car on the interstate, someone had come after him, and he was driving a friend's car home. Marty certainly didn't need this extra disaster when he was trying to get to Liberty to be with us.

Fritz: The pastor of First United Methodist Church in Blue Springs called to offer their sanctuary as the place for the Service of Death and Resurrection. At the time, churches still were reluctant to host services for a person who had died of AIDS. This act of hospitality endeared the congregation to us even more. It also helped us come to a decision regarding the location of a memorial service in the Kansas City area. We had served this congregation from 1982 until 1987. In my current position as district superintendent, I related to more than fifty congregations. The invitation from Blue Springs relieved us of the chore of choosing between churches in the district I served.

Etta Mae: We returned to Kansas City on Saturday. Because of the Christmas holiday on Tuesday, we did not schedule the second service until the following Thursday. This allowed time to arrange for a visitation on Wednesday evening, but the delay meant we had to wait a long time for liturgical closure.

Waiting for us when we arrived back from Atlanta was a refrigerator full of food and a cross-stitch picture from Sue Ann Greer. The picture showed two friends embracing and the words read, "You need a hug." She couldn't be there when we arrived, but the picture showed how she felt. The picture still hangs on our wall as a reminder that everyone needs many, many hugs.

Fritz: Our bishop, W. T. Handy, Jr., ministered at the service with grace and dignity, giving words of affirmation and consolation.

Music was an important part of the celebration. The congregation sang hymns of faith, and the church choir presented an anthem. Tim had been a soloist and a fine musician. He enjoyed singing with the Gay Men's Chorus in Atlanta. At one of their performances he sang "Silent Night" in German as a solo. Since Bart had that solo on tape, he requested that we play it during the service. There was not a dry eye in the sanctuary after that solo. It was such a touching addition to the service.

Etta Mae: The other soloist, Holly Wood, sang, at Tim's request, "Bless the Beasts and the Children." We had not told her about Tim's taped solo, and it had moved her deeply. She struggled to gain control of her emotions so she could make it through her own solo.

Patty Ryle Clay, a seminary classmate and close friend, preached the sermon. Tim had asked her more than a year before to bring this message.

In her sermon, she said, "Tim was . . . a *quiet* enabler, an encourager, someone who was *for* you in the deepest sense of the word as an advocate and fellow sojourner. He was full of wisdom and understanding." A portion of her sermon is excerpted here.

Tim's life reflected many fine qualities but perhaps the best were his courage, his concern with injustice, and his personal integrity. Which is why a memorial service for him would be amiss and dishonest if it didn't testify to the fact that Tim was gay and that he died with AIDS.

His parents said they wanted everyone to know he died of AIDS, and I'm sure a big part of that motivation was to create openness and help others who have it or who have a family member with it to be able to talk about and deal with it. AIDS is such a cruel disease; it doesn't need the shame and isolation from others to make it even more cruel.

But just as there was no room in the inn for Jesus, in many ways there was no room in the church for Tim.

Surely God would not have it so—who in the form of a human being taught us how to reach out and touch and heal and be with ones who are deathly sick and at the same time are cast out and made exiles by society. We as Christ's church should be different, for Jesus our brother, strong and good, has shown us the Way of love and compassion and of acceptance.

17

A FAMILY IN MOURNING

O God, I bring before you this day:

My weakness for your strength.
My sins and my failings for your forgiveness.
My duties, my ambitions, and my hopes for your help.
My loved ones, my family, and those dear to me
*   for your protection.*
My dreams, my ambitions, my aims and my hopes
*   for your blessing.*

Now in this moment give me:

Strength to live with the weight laid upon me.
Wisdom in my speaking or in my silence.
Gentleness in my actions.
Peace within my heart and soul.

Search me and know me.
And so bring me to end this day in contentment,
*   in happiness, and in goodness.*
Through Jesus Christ my Lord. Amen.[*]

Fritz: Fred had a hard time with the service for Tim. It forced Fred into a new awareness that he, too, was very seriously ill and that this was a death-dealing virus he carried in his body.

He flew back to New York right after the funeral; in fact, some friends took him to the airport directly from the church. It was so hard to see him go, especially when he cried and held on to his mother tightly. None of us wanted to let go.

Etta Mae: Just a few days after Tim's funeral, I went to the shopping center to make some purchases. As I drove through a green light, I suddenly realized that traffic was stopped ahead of me. It was too late to stop, even though I applied my brakes. I hit the rear end of a pickup, and pushed him into the car in front of him. No tickets were issued as it was cold and some ice patches were still on the pavement. However, looking back, I'm sure my mind was not where it should have been, and probably the accident could have been avoided. My stress level increased tremendously as I sat there waiting for the police to arrive and investigate. I called Fritz to come and be with me, something I would normally not have done. I pride myself on handling challenging situations calmly and confidently. I certainly didn't feel calm or confident then.

The accident caused considerable damage to our car (but not much to the pickup or the other car), and the body shop indicated it would be two to three weeks before it would be ready to drive again. In the meantime, what were we to do for a car to get me to work? The insurance company would pay for a rental car for only five days, and we needed one longer than that.

The Chief of Police of Kansas City, Larry Joiner, happened to be a member of the Avondale church where I worked. When he and Dorothy heard about my accident, they offered a car of theirs that wasn't being driven by anyone. We jumped at the chance to borrow it. Fritz decided to drive it to work, and I would drive his car.

Fritz: There was still ice and snow on the ground, and the driveway to my office parking lot was very steep. Therefore, we all parked our cars on a side street close to the building. When I left for home after work, the first day I had driven Larry's car, I noticed it was not parked as I had left it. Then I saw a police officer standing nearby. There had been a hit-and-run accident, and Larry's car had been rammed! I told the officer it wasn't even my car and that it belonged to Larry Joiner. The officer said, "*The* Larry Joiner?" When I said yes, he said he was glad I was the one who had borrowed it instead of himself! That was the only funny thing about the whole episode.

Larry Joiner is a very kind person, and he told us not to worry about the accident. However, this was just one more stress point in our lives at a time when we were grieving over the loss of Tim.

Etta Mae: We made sure Fred got back to Kansas City every two to three months so we could monitor his progress or decline. He came home in the spring of 1991 for a short visit. During that time, his temperature shot up again and we called his doctor in New York. The doctor said to put him in the hospital in Missouri for immediate treatment. We did that, but it was an unhappy time for all of us.

The staff at this particular hospital did not know how to care for AIDS patients. They displayed their fear to us and Fred. They put a "Contamination" sign outside the door. Fred indicated that was unnecessary; it could have been placed just inside where only the nurses would see it. Even the doctor was curt and stayed only as long as necessary. After two days of that, Fred said he was getting out of that hospital, and we agreed it would be best.

We told the doctor of Fred's decision, and the doctor said he would not release Fred because he was too ill. Once again, we called the doctor in New York. He said to take Fred from the hospital, put him on a flight to New York, and have him go directly to St. Vincent's Hospital from the airport—he was not to stop at home on the way. Fred agreed to this, and we informed the Missouri doctor of our plans. He still said he would not agree unless Fred signed a release saying he took the full responsibility himself. Fred was only too glad to do so. He checked out as quickly as possible, flew to New York, and spent a few more days at St. Vincent's recovering.

There was one good experience before Fred left the Missouri hospital: friends brought him pizza from his favorite pizza place. They delivered it to his hospital room and enjoyed eating it with him.

Fritz: Fred enjoyed life as much as he could with his limited capabilities. He loved the botanical gardens in Brooklyn's Prospect Park. They were located only about a mile or so from his apartment. Friends pushed him there in his wheelchair often so he could see the unusual flowers.

In July of 1991, we were scheduled to take a three-week trip to Hong Kong, Singapore, and China. Just a week or so before we were to leave, Fred called to say he was in the hospital. He said he was doing all right, and we were not to worry. We do not remember the cause for the trip to the hospital; it was probably another battle with PCP. He sounded good over the phone, so we assumed he was telling us all we needed to know. Still we wondered if we should cancel our trip; it would be almost impossible for us to get back if something serious occurred. Fred encouraged us to go ahead with our trip; he assured us he was doing fine. We asked, "Would you tell us if you weren't?" "No!" he said. "Now go on to China."

Neither of us felt comfortable leaving the country without checking on Fred personally, so we flew to New York to visit him. It was a relief to see him in good spirits. He told us that the nurses had a party in his room almost every night. Just being with him was a party. One day he and Rocky made a game of working the electric controls on the bed. They would both get in the bed and push both the head and foot buttons until they were squeezed in between. It was such fun to watch them *enjoying* a hospital stay.

Etta Mae: As we relished this visit, we also took time to process some of our feelings about Tim's death. Time was so limited on the occasion of the funeral that we had only begun to work on our grief. We talked over the phone frequently to Fred, but this was no substitute for a face-to-face visit.

In some ways we all began the grieving process when we first learned that both Tim and Fred were infected with HIV. At first we denied it, but then we admitted that AIDS is a terminal illness. Anger never got us down. We felt no need to blame our sons for getting sick. We did not blame God, who we always knew as a loving, sustaining presence. We prayed to God, begging for a cure, longing for the gift of more time. Probably we bargained with God, offering somehow to change our lives if these petitions could be answered. We accepted the realities of living with AIDS and counted on God, our family, loved ones, and friends to stand with us through the ordeal.

Tim's death put the grieving into a new context. Now he was gone. There was a great hole in our lives that could never be filled again. Tears helped. Talking helped even more. We told our story to everyone who would listen. We repeated the details in therapeutic regimen.

Fritz: I would not admit it, but the sorrow took a terrible toll. I tried to be strong and go on with life, but I was slipping deeper into depression. I couldn't sleep through until morning. I never had any trouble going to sleep, but I would wake up at 2:30 A.M. and stay awake the rest of the night. My body wore down. My heart was breaking. I finally sought medical help and was told it was a classic case of depression. Medication was prescribed, and it at least helped me sleep through the night. My heart, however, was not healed.

Etta Mae: Marty seldom expressed his feelings. We often encouraged him to talk, but he found it difficult to put his feelings into words. He did voice his regrets that he never got to tell Tim good-bye. He said he wished that he had had the opportunity to talk with him one more time before Tim's death came. He was wanting more times when just he, Tim, and Fred sat together and talked about life and what was happening to them. They would gather in the basement or the garage or one of the bedrooms for conversation, and now those times were gone.

We could only imagine how the pain of losing a brother loaded him down. A big part of his life was missing.

---

* Patricia D. Brown, in Patricia D. Brown and T. Todd Masman, eds., *Meditations for HIV and AIDS Ministries* (Health and Welfare Ministries Program Department, General Board of Global Ministries, The United Methodist Church, 1993), p. 55.

18

MOVING TO FLORIDA

The LORD is my shepherd;
I have everything I need.
He lets me rest in fields of green grass
and leads me to quiet pools of fresh water.
He gives me new strength.
He guides me in the right paths,
as he has promised.
Even if I go through the deepest darkness,
I will not be afraid, LORD,
for you are with me.
Your shepherd's rod and staff protect me.

You prepare a banquet for me,
where all my enemies can see me;
you welcome me as an honored guest
and fill my cup to the brim.
I know that your goodness and love will be with me all
my life;
and your house will be my home as long as I live.
—Psalm 23

Fritz: While we were in New York, Fred threw us another bombshell. No, he wasn't going back to Alaska; he was moving to Florida! Florida? Why had he chosen to leave New York, a place he could hardly wait to live in when he was twenty years old? He said, "New York is dirty and it doesn't have any trees and flowers close to where we are. It is all cement. I want to live in an area where I can lie outside in the sunshine and breathe fresh, clean air."

We talked to his doctor, who told us it would be a very bad decision on Fred's part to move. He reminded Fred that he had been his doctor all the way through this and knew what was going on in Fred's body. He also reminded Fred that he had many, many friends in New York and it would be a mistake psychologically to move away from them to a place where he knew no one.

He was right about those friends. A large circle of men and women supported him throughout his illness. Every time he was in the hospital, six, eight, ten of them would come to see him. They staggered their visits so that he had company many hours every day. We marveled at the care they showed him and at the never-ending loyalty they had to him. Many were people of no religious faith, yet they exhibited Christianity at its best.

Etta Mae: That old stubbornness came out in Fred when we discouraged his move; he was determined to move to Florida. In fact, he and Rocky had already rented a condominium there and planned to move over Labor Day. Knowing further discussion was useless, we gave our blessing.

We invited them to come through Kansas City on their way to Florida. As an incentive, we offered to give them a car. We had provided cars for Tim and Marty when they graduated from college, but no one in their right mind would have a car in New York City. So Fred had depended on public transportation for the nine years he had lived there. We knew he would need a car in Florida, and we wanted to give him one of ours.

Such a change we saw in Fred in September. It was unbelievable how he had wasted away since our visit to New York in July. His arms and legs were like toothpicks. He slept most of the time, day and night. We had to wake him for meals. He had to sleep on a foam "egg-carton" mattress and had to put pillows between his legs to keep his knee bones from rubbing together. Also, he had no appetite. It was a terrible shock after seeing him doing so well just two months before.

Fritz: We suggested that Rocky and I drive the car to Florida. Fred and Etta Mae could fly down after we got there. But, no, Fred was going in the car with Rocky—end of conversation. He wanted to be there when the furniture arrived.

We sent them off to Florida, and once again, that feeling emerged that we would not see Fred alive again. How many times had we gone through this?

We asked that they call from the home of Jay Krumeich and Holly Wood, where they planned to spend the first night. But we didn't hear from them. We called Jay and Holly the next morning. Yes, Fred and Rocky had been there and had gone on. They both expressed their concern for the way Fred looked and acted. We didn't hear from Fred and Rocky for three days, but they finally called and said they had arrived in Florida and were staying with a friend.

Etta Mae: Somewhere, either at our house or in Florida, Fred contracted toxoplasmosis, another opportunistic infection that invades the tissues and may seriously damage the central nervous system. Since the disease may be transmitted by cats or litter boxes, we assume he may have gotten it from our family pet. However, Fred had no contact with our cat as far as we knew. Kittles was so heavy, at seventeen pounds, that Fred did not want him in his lap.

Toxoplasmosis may cause loss of memory. Fred experienced this shortly after he moved to Florida. He couldn't remember who anyone was, including Rocky at times, although he always knew who we were when we called.

We had always dreaded the possibility of dementia. For many persons living with AIDS, the loss of mental capabilities is the final and most humiliating symptom. How glad we were that Tim never suffered from dementia. How we hoped that Fred never would.

TOXOPLASMOSIS: Toxoplasmosis, transmitted hand to mouth primarily from cat feces, is a common infection with very few symptoms in most segments of the population. In AIDS, toxoplasmosis tends to be more severe, causing an inflammation of the brain with fevers, changes in ability to move, and personality or behavior changes. (Taken from *LIVING WITH AIDS: A Self-Care Manual*, a publication of AIDS Project Los Angeles)

Also, from a pamphlet that was handed out at a workshop we attended was this explanation:

Toxoplasmosis: A disease due to infection with the protozoa *Toxoplasma gondii*, frequently causing focal encephalitis (inflammation of the brain). Toxoplasmosis may also involve the heart, lung, adrenals, pancreas, and testes.

Fred never got out of his bed after arriving in Florida. He never got to enjoy that green grass and fresh air he anticipated. We doubt he even knew he had moved to Florida. One day he said to us, "I get to go home tomorrow." (He was in his own condo.) "Where is home?" we asked. "I don't know," he answered. "But it isn't here." How our hearts ached for him! How sad to see a fine, healthy, intelligent young man waste away physically and mentally. How terrible it is when that young man is your son.

19

ANOTHER SON'S DEATH

O God, I wasn't there for him!
Why didn't you let me be there for him?
When he walked through
the valley of the shadow of death,
I wasn't there to hold him
against the night of fear
or to comfort him
in the atrocity of his pain.
O God, you could have given me that!
You could have allowed me
to be with him in his hour.

When you called my name,
didn't I come?
And didn't I stay?
Haven't I spent my life
searching for your truth?
O God, where was our covenant
that night?
Where, O God, were you?
What's the sense of all this,
O Mystery?
What's the sense
of all my pain?
What good comes from
my tears?
What is better because
he died?
What is better because
I cried?
The world still spits in
the eye of God.

This is my prayer, O Holy One:
Give me the peace
that passes
understanding.
Give me the assurance
that you were
there for him.
Give me the assurance
that you are here
for me.

O God, in your mysterious power
you make the oceans roar
and the starfish
wash upon the shore.
And my son lives
in the heart of heaven,
and I live
in the heart of earth,
but we live together
in the heart of God.*

Etta Mae: On a Friday morning, three weeks after Fred had moved to Florida, Rocky called to say Fred was having a seizure. He had called 911 and the paramedics were working on Fred. Rocky said as soon as they got Fred stabilized he would call Fritz back at his office.

I furiously set to work printing the church bulletin so I would be free to fly to Lakeland to be with Fred. I was running the copy machine when I turned around and saw Fritz come through the door. I knew immediately that Rocky had called and what the message was. I began yelling, "No, no, no. I wanted to see him before he died." But Fred was gone. The paramedics attributed his death to cardiac arrest.

Fred was twenty-nine years old when he died, on September 20, 1991.

Fritz: We had tried in that half-hour time span to schedule a flight to Lakeland, but we were too late. We agonized that we had not been present. How we wanted to be with him in his last hours.

Two sons dead! HIV had won the second battle too. As the truth soaked in, our tears ran again. We held each other and confessed we were too numb to take next steps.

Etta Mae: My boss and friend, Dave Finestead, heard my cries and came out to be with us. He took us to the privacy of his office, where we prayed with him for strength to handle another death. We called our good friend Carl Martin, in Winfield, and asked him if he would go to the radio station and break the news to Marty that another brother had died. We also requested that Carl take Marty home and stay with him awhile, and he did. Marty immediately packed his bags and started on the long drive to Liberty. Since it was a four-hour trip, Marty had time to grieve alone—an important issue for him, he later told us.

Fritz: Of course there were other things to do. We had to call our mothers and tell them that another grandson was dead. We had to get the word to other family members and to friends.

Decisions needed to be made concerning the funeral arrangements. Should we go to Florida? Rocky said he did not need us to come. He offered to call a mortuary and arrange to have the body shipped to Kansas City. He would come to Kansas City at the same time, and together we would plan for a service.

* Ann Weems, *Psalms of Lament* (Louisville: Westminster John Knox Press, 1995), pp. 101-2.

20

CELEBRATING DEATH AND RESURRECTION II

[Jesus said,] "Do not let your hearts be troubled. Believe in God, believe also in me. In my Father's house there are many dwelling places. If it were not so, would I have told you that I go to prepare a place for you? And if I go and prepare a place for you, I will come again and will take you to myself, so that where I am, there you may be also. And you know the way to the place where I am going."
—John 14:1-4 NRSV

Etta Mae: Fred did not want to be cremated. He wanted to be buried in a *solid gold* casket. "Who's going to pay for it," we kidded, "and who's going to carry it?" He had a wonderful sense of humor and very expensive tastes.

Where, then, should his body be buried? Next to us, we decided. But we had no plot for our own burials. We had to select a place. It did not make sense to have our final resting place in our hometown since we no longer had ties there. What did seem reasonable was to choose a location in the area where we had lived for nearly twenty years, the area where we expected to retire. We purchased three lots at a cemetery in Kansas City North—one for Fred, one for Fritz, and one for me.

Dave Finestead, pastor at Avondale United Methodist Church, where I was employed as secretary, called to suggest that the Service of Death and Resurrection be held at Avondale. We were grateful for the offer.

A visitation was scheduled for Sunday evening. The worship service was set for Monday, following an interment service at the cemetery, attended by family and close friends.

Fritz: Bishop W. T. Handy, Jr., who had been a source of encouragement and strength for us through both illnesses, presided at the service.

Music provided a witness to our faith. Holly Wood sang a selection from Handel's *Messiah*. A quartet of district superintendents— sang "Precious Lord, Take My Hand."

The preacher was Cathie Lyons, Assistant General Secretary, Department of Health and Welfare Ministries, the General Board of Global Ministries of The United Methodist Church. I had first met her at the National Consultation on AIDS Ministries in 1987. After Tim and Fred became ill, she and I shared leadership roles at a workshop in the Kansas East Conference.

Cathie offered us personal support throughout Fred's illness. She visited Fred nearly every time he went to the hospital. They got to be good friends, enjoying social occasions as well as times of crisis. It was natural that she deliver a message of remembrance and celebration.

Cathie painted a word picture of Fred for the many persons who attended the service. She spoke as if only our immediate family were in the room:

> Fred's pleasure was in things other than sports, and as parents you encouraged him in the direction of his heart's desires. He took delight in music and sang with the Gay Men's Chorus in New York City. He appreciated fine fabric and clothing design, and he studied to be a designer. Fred loved to cook, and as a boy growing up he was permitted to feel at home in the kitchen. One Saturday as he prepared chicken and dumplings and cheese cake for Rocky and me and another friend, he walked around the kitchen telling us about you and all you had taught him, Etta Mae. Later that evening he sat on the couch with that wonderful family picture album balanced precariously on his thin legs. He took us through every picture telling us about his grandmas, about Halloween costumes, the different places you lived, the churches you served, Fritz. In those pictures we saw a family together—parents, sons, grandparents—a family filled with happiness and hopes and aspirations before the word *AIDS* ever entered our vocabulary.

After the family photo album came the presentation of the stuffed dolls (one of Fred and one of Rocky) wearing their christening dresses. The stuffed dolls—in dresses, booties, caps and all—brought such pleasure and joy at evening's end. We laughed until we cried. Laughter, humor, a sense of perspective: they were so important as the walls of illness closed in around us.

Etta Mae: In the sermon, Cathie spoke directly to Fred's grandmothers and to his brother, Marty. This special care for Marty touched a concern that many people raise. They want to know how Marty coped with the death of two brothers. We believe he handled it with mature strength, but we confess that it was difficult to get Marty to talk about our losses. In the intervening years, all of us have learned how to express our feelings and use them for healing. One of the ways Marty has helped us is to keep us laughing. The pain is still severe, but Marty's sense of humor helps us keep smiling through the tears.

Fritz: As the months passed following the second death, we uncovered an issue we had assumed would not be important. The cemetery gave us a place to rehearse memories of Fred. Because Tim's body had been cremated, there was no place to memorialize him. Part of Tim's ashes had been scattered, as he requested, at a special place in the Great Smoky Mountains, and the remainder had been scattered on the surf at Key West.

Etta Mae: So, we had a grave site for Fred, but nothing for Tim. There was a very real void in our lives, something we had not considered when we sat down with Tim to make arrangements for his funeral. We talked a long time about what we could do to fill that emptiness. We conferred with the funeral home, and they suggested that we could have Tim's name printed on a memorial wall, within their cemetery boundaries. That didn't seem to be quite what we wanted, so we asked if they could just make us a new marker. They agreed to replace the plaque on the grave site with a new one. The marker now has both Tim's and Fred's names on it with a small banner saying "Brothers" across the middle. It is very satisfying to us.

It would have been helpful to us if we had discussed these matters with someone who had experienced the cremation of a loved one. We had talked with Tim about who he wanted to participate in his service and what he wanted done with his body. However, none of those discussions took place with Fred. He didn't seem to feel comfortable talking about that, feeling as he did that he was going to lick this illness. We do think the service we planned would have pleased him, even without the gold casket!

21

FRIENDS CARE

Two simple words. I care. What more could I say or do? I have given all I have to give. I have laughed with her. I have cried with her. I have held her in my arms. I have let her go.

How could I have thought this would be easy? Just a few hours a month they said. Now it is a few hours a day, filled with shopping, cleaning, cooking, feeding, helping. Where will I find the strength to go on?[*]

Fritz: A huge circle of caring friends and colleagues surrounded us during this awful journey through AIDS. We have already provided numerous illustrations of this care. Now we want to recount just a few more of these instances of supportive friendship.

The congregation of our former parish in Blue Springs offered a series of caring deeds. It started before we knew that either son was HIV-positive.

In 1986 or 1987, Fred developed a growth in the back of his mouth. When he called to tell us about it, the doctors had no diagnosis. They would watch it for a while to see what happened. Immediate fears of cancer sprung up in our minds. We shared our concern with the congregation on Sunday morning and asked for prayers. One church member offered more than prayers; he offered his credit card and told us to go to New York at once to see Fred. We were to use his credit card for anything we needed—housing, medicine, airfare, anything. We were glad that the growth went away and we did not need to accept, but it was a loving gesture.

In this same church, a Sunday school class put Tim and Fred on their prayer list. They sent cards regularly and called to keep updated. Once when we called to express appreciation, I brought the class up to date on the progress of their illnesses. I happened to mention that I had gone to the pharmacy with Fred to pick up a prescription for AZT. It provided a three-week supply and cost more than $600. In a few days, a check for $600 came from the Sunday school class. The note said, "Use this to help defray the cost of medications." Every few weeks after that another check arrived.

Etta Mae: From another local church, a person brought Fred a video tape of Alaska, knowing he was going there in a few days. Another woman called to see what she could bring Fred to eat. When he said "pie," she asked what kind. He mentioned two of his favorites, either of which would be wonderful. When she arrived, she had two pies—one of each of his favorites. A local church called to see what they could do for us or Tim and Fred when they were hospitalized. Both sons requested live flowers in their rooms, and they were provided by that church.

Fritz: Not only did friends in local congregations care, but so did colleagues in our denominational connection. On that occasion when Fred was hospitalized during a meeting of the General Board of Global Ministries, I had responsibility for leading worship one morning. During that service I shared our story. Afterwards, scores of persons surrounded me and offered their support.

During our long stay in New York in May of 1990, we called the General Board of Global Ministries and said we were in New York alone with no support. It came immediately in the way of transportation for us, calls at the hospital, and being taken out for meals. The General Secretary, Randolph Nugent, and several staff members visited Fred in the hospital. Three bishops and two district superintendents called on him. Later, when Fred was released from the hospital, these friends arranged for a cab to take him home. They continued to call him throughout his illness.

We found comfort worshiping at Metropolitan Duane United Methodist Church, which is located across the street from St. Vincent's Hospital. The pastor ministered to us and to Fred. One Sunday there was a guest preacher from New Jersey in the pulpit. We introduced ourselves but shared nothing of our story. That afternoon the guest preacher Hae-Jong Kim (now Bishop of the Pittsburgh Area) and his wife, Wha-Sei, came to make a pastoral call on Fred and us, bringing along a bouquet of flowers, something Fred loved.

Etta Mae: After Fred's death, our good friend Don Messer called to check on us. He wanted to lend a helping hand in some way. He wondered if a few days of retreat at a condominium available to the seminary would be helpful. It was at our disposal any time we wanted to use it, he said.

At one point, I almost took advantage of his offer by myself. I desperately needed to hide and went so far as to check on airline passage and the availability of the condo. Then I decided I needed Fritz with me, so I put the idea aside for a later time. Later we drove to Denver together and found retreat and renewal. We are grateful to Don for that offer.

Fritz: Another friend named Don called shortly after Fred's death. Don Ott, now a retired United Methodist Bishop, called to make an amazing offer. He knew that I would soon be engaged in the fall round of charge conferences. As a district superintendent, I had the responsibility of presiding at nearly fifty of these charge conferences, which are annual meetings of congregations within the bounds of the district I served. Don offered to come to Missouri and preside at all of those charge conferences.

That offer made us realize how much he cared about our well-being. At that time he, himself, was a district superintendent. He would soon be facing a round of charge conferences in his own district. We do not know who was going to cover for him in Wisconsin, but it truly was an extravagant offer! I declined his offer, but Don's spirit was with me at every one of those charge conferences that fall.

There were other symbolic acts that carried enormous significance. May Chun's gifts were extraordinary. On the day that I led worship at the World Division of the General Board of Global Ministries, one of the first colleagues to respond was May Chun. She wrapped me in a comforting hug and promised to pray for us regularly. Six months later, after Tim's death, she greeted me at the spring meeting of the Board.

"Yesterday, before I left home in Hawaii," she said, "I had a boy carry a lei out on the surf and set it afloat. It is our custom to do this when we mourn the loss of someone's life. We did this in memory of your son, Tim."

At the fall meeting, following Fred's death, May came to me

again. This time she reported, "We planted a tree in Fred's memory last week. We wanted a living memorial to his life and witness." It gave us the idea of doing the same thing. We planted a blue spruce tree in our yard in Topeka in memory of both Tim and Fred.

Etta Mae: One of my very closest friends, Donna Hoover, showed me what real friendship means when she offered to go to New York with me. Fred was seriously ill, and we weren't sure if Fritz would be able to make the trip. I decided I was going, but was dreading going by myself to the "big city." When I conveyed this to Donna, she said, "I'll go with you." I mentioned that it was terribly expensive, especially on short notice, that I would be staying at Fred's apartment and sleeping on an air mattress on the floor, and that I had no idea how long I would need to be there. Her reply was, "I will pay my own way. I can sleep on the floor as well as you can, and I can stay as long as you need me." Needless to say, I was touched beyond words.

We also experienced the enormous support of friends surrounding us when we shared (after the deaths of Tim and Fred) about having a granddaughter. Their responses were almost unanimous: "Some of Fred is still living!"

Siobhan Marie Williams was born in January 1983 and lives with her mother. She is a brilliant, talented, and beautiful person. We discover anew each time we are with her how many of Fred's talents she has inherited. Music and the arts seem to be her forte, as well as an intelligent mind. Fred exhibited those qualities, also, and we delight in seeing the resemblance. We occasionally notice the similarities in their eyes, their personalities, and their actions. We are grateful to be a part of her life, knowing how enriched our lives have become because of her. Our lives will forever intertwine, and we are proud to call her our granddaughter.

* T. Todd Masman, in Patricia D. Brown and T. Todd Masman, eds. *Meditations for HIV and AIDS Ministries* (Health and Welfare Ministries Program Department, General Board of Global Ministries, The United Methodist Church, 1993), p. 18.

22

IN MEMORY OF

Fritz: Two booklets published by the General Board of Global Ministries have special meaning for us. One is entitled *Worship Resources for HIV and AIDS Ministries* by Patricia D. Brown and Adele K. Wilcox. It came into print through the efforts of Cathie Lyons.

In October, after Fred's funeral, I had returned to New York for the fall board meeting. I met Cathie in the hotel lobby. "Come here," she said, "I want to show you something." It was a copy of the worship resource.

She told me that the day we called to notify her of Fred's death, the galley proofs for the booklet had just been delivered to her desk. She immediately asked the publisher, "Could we put one more page in this book before it is printed?" The publisher agreed, copy was developed, and a dedication page was included. This is how it reads:

This worship resource
for HIV/AIDS ministries
is dedicated to the memory and lives
of Fred and Tim Mutti,
who died from the complications of AIDS,
to their loving and courageous parents,
Etta Mae and Fritz Mutti,
and their brother, Marty

and to all mothers and fathers, sons and
daughters,
brothers and sisters, husbands and wives,
companions, loved ones and friends whose
lives had been touched by HIV and AIDS.*

Etta Mae: We are deeply grateful for this kind remembrance.
That page symbolizes the tremendous support given to us in hundreds and hundreds of ways.

Fritz: Another resource that is important to us is *Meditations for HIV and AIDS Ministries,* edited by Patricia D. Brown and T. Todd Masman. The General Board of Global Ministries also published this booklet.

There is a cross on the front that is made up of names. The very first names are Fritz, Etta Mae, Fred, Tim, and Marty. In a very special way our story is memorialized in these two documents. Through them we have a significant spiritual connection to all those who use them in ministry to and for persons living with AIDS.

Etta Mae: Because we are well known across the church, we have received care that countless hundreds do not receive. We are humbled, but we also know that every person struggling in the face of this dreadful disease deserves the same care and support. We pray that it will be so.

THE CHURCH PRAYS

Every church can have a prayer ministry reaching out to, and supporting, persons living with AIDS and their loved ones. *Worship Resources for HIV and AIDS Ministries* and *Meditations for HIV and AIDS Ministries* may serve as important resources to a church's ministry of prayer.

Names can be lifted up during the prayers in a regular worship service.

A prayer group can be organized; it needs only three or four persons participating to be effective. On a regular schedule this group can come together, follow the basic worship pattern, sing hymns, lift names, and offer prayers of petition and intercession.

It is so simple, you would think that every church would have such a prayer ministry already.

---

* Patricia D. Brown and Adele K. Wilcox, *Worship Resources for HIV and AIDS Ministries* (General Board of Global Ministries, The United Methodist Church, 1991), p. v.

23

THE MUTTI AIDS FUND

Many, many people came to visit us, telephoned, or sent cards. Many wanted to contribute to a memorial fund. We decided to establish a fund with the Department of Health and Welfare Ministries of the Board of Global Ministries, and we call it the Mutti AIDS Fund.

Proceeds from this fund go to HIV/AIDS ministries throughout the United States where they assist in the development of new programs of education, outreach, and direct support while they continue and strengthen vital HIV/AIDS programs relied upon by those infected with and affected by HIV. We especially wanted some grants to assist families with emergency needs.

Travel expenses can reach enormous totals for families wanting to be near a loved one in trauma. Our situation was unique in that we had two sons living with AIDS at the same time. To be with them, we made frequent trips to New York and Atlanta. Sometimes one of us went to one city and the other traveled to the other city. Many persons need assistance with the burden of travel costs.

Other expenses, such as lodging costs or special equipment needs, may push persons beyond their limits. While our fund cannot meet huge demands, like medications not covered by insurance, we hope that some limited assistance can be offered to individuals or church groups.

Several thousands of dollars have been granted to applicants since the Fund was established. At one time we noted that grants had gone to provide seed money for several "Strength for the Journey Retreats" for men and women living with HIV/AIDS. Other grants went to Chicago; Johnson City, Tennessee; New York; Dayton; Atlanta; Allentown; Worcester, Massachusetts; San Francisco; Denver; York, Pennsylvania; Melbourne, Florida; and New Orleans.

We are grateful to those who have made contributions and pray that donors will continue to underwrite this important ministry.

How Do I Contribute?

It's simple:
1) **Make your check payable to:**
Mutti AIDS Fund

2)**Send it to:**
Mutti AIDS Fund
c/o Health and Welfare Ministries
General Board of Global Ministries
475 Riverside Drive
New York, NY 10115

(Telephone: 212/870-3871)

24

LIFE STORIES IN THREE-BY-SIX PANELS

Common threads
Tugging, through
Life's fabric

Joy and pain
Anxiety and celebration
Woven through
a common story

Unique lives
Diverse commitments
Come together
in shared pain

Ordinary people
Extraordinary circumstances
Called to experience
uncommon loss

Deep emotion
Tugging, pulling
Moving through
*Common threads**

Fritz: The Names Project AIDS Memorial Quilt serves a unique role in the battle against AIDS. Three-by-six-foot panels honor those who have died of AIDS and reach out through community displays to encourage both compassion and personal involvement.

Recently, at an AIDS Conference in Kansas, hosted by the Area AIDS Task Force, one of our keynote speakers was Cleve Jones, the founder of the NAMES Project AIDS Memorial Quilt. During his speech he shared with us how the first panel was created.

Cleve and his friends saw this disease rage through their communities, and friend after friend died because of complications related to AIDS. Cleve believed a response was needed. He led candlelight marches. He went to conferences. He pleaded with community leaders to take action, and he passed out brochures. Then in 1985, Cleve himself tested positive for HIV. He no longer was just carrying the banner for his friends; he was carrying the banner for himself, too.

As Cleve was planning an annual candlelight march in 1985, he learned that the number of people in San Francisco alone who had lost their lives to AIDS had passed the one-thousand mark. So he asked each person who was taking part in the candlelight march to write the names of their friends and loved ones who had died of AIDS on placards. At the end of the march, Cleve and the others stood on ladders, above a candlelight sea, taping the names to the wall of the San Francisco Federal Building. The wall of placards looked to Cleve like a patchwork quilt.

Cleve was inspired by this sight, and he made plans for a larger memorial. About a year later he created the first panel in memory of his friend, Marvin Feldman. In June of 1987, Cleve teamed up with several others to formally organize the NAMES Project Foundation. Individuals created panels to be sewn together in the manner of a patchwork quilt. Each panel was to be three feet by six feet, the same size as a covering for a casket. As of this writing, there are 41,000 panels, and the size now prohibits the exhibit of the entire quilt in one place.

Etta Mae: We knew about the quilt project, of course, before Tim and Fred died, and Tim had mentioned to me that he would like for me to make one for him. Fred seemed nonchalant about the matter.

I did decide to take on this project, but how does one tell a son's story with a three-by-six-foot piece of cloth? What a struggle I had with this!

I was not mentally ready to start this project for the first year after Fred died. It was difficult making decisions. What symbols did I want to use? Would there be a theme? What colors would I use? Nothing seemed to come together. I would begin; then I would have to put it away for awhile. I would ask people what they thought should go on the panel, and invariably I would discard their ideas. I even asked my friend Donna Hoover to help me with a theme, and we spent an afternoon together, discussing, drawing, erasing, drawing some more. I still wasn't satisfied when we parted.

It finally dawned on me that this had to be *my* project if I were to be satisfied with the final product. Once that decision was made, it was much easier for me to begin, to hibernate for hours at a time, trying to decide what to do.

Tim and Fred were two such different people and yet were bound together tightly because of the pain they both went through. Still, the panels had to be separate—one panel for both just would not work for me. So, I began working on two panels— one for Tim and one for Fred. One symbol for Tim was a piano, since he was a fine musician. I had known for quite sometime— before I began thinking of a theme—that I wanted to put a piano on Tim's panel. I found a pattern and I cross-stitched that symbol for him. I was pleased with the work when it was finished. Fred had told me several times that he really liked the poem "Footprints in the Sand," so that cross-stitch was done for Fred's panel.

Those were the two easiest symbols I did. In trying to make the panels "perfect" I started over several times. I would think to myself, "Tim would have done this so much better" or "Fred's drawings would be so much better than mine," and I would discard what I had done and begin again. I was trying to be a wonderful artist, as Tim and Fred had been, and it took me awhile to realize these panels were not going to come out like their work. They would represent only my work. Fritz was such an encourager and supporter; he kept telling me that what I was doing or had done was just what it should be. Perhaps I spent all this time on the panels and started over so often as a way to postpone making the final decisions. Being finished with the panels indicated some closure on Tim's and Fred's lives, and I wasn't ready for closure.

Fritz: Etta Mae chose symbols of hope and symbols indicative of Tim's and Fred's personalities. Since Tim was a wonderful musician, there is a music staff for the background, plus the piano. Then there was a palette for his artistic abilities, a graduation cap for his outstanding academic record and his commitment to teaching, and a drawing of an adult surrounded by little ones for his work with children.

For Fred, we had the everlasting symbol of hope with the word *Alaska*. We also found some of the designs that he created while at the Fashion Institute of Technology, and we chose one of those for his quilt. Then a picture that says, "I just have to be me." That described his personality perfectly!

Etta Mae: It took me about six months before I was satisfied with the way the panels looked. In February 1993 we presented the panels while the AIDS quilt was on display in Topeka. We celebrated this presentation by inviting close friends to the ceremony, then to our home for refreshments and visiting. It was a healing time for me. My family had been with us that weekend to celebrate my mother's eightieth birthday, but only one brother and his wife were able to stay for the panel presentation.

By the time the panels were finished, even Fritz had become attached to them and suggested we just keep them and hang them in the basement. However, they were shipped off to San Francisco, where they joined the thousands of others being taken care of in the NAMES Project warehouse. The one request we made of the NAMES Project was that they keep the panels together. They accommodated us, and the panels are sewn together in one of the squares.

---

* Jeanette Willis Fagerberg, in *Alive Now!* January/February 1993, The Upper Room.

25

THE STRUGGLE AGAINST JUDGMENT AND HATRED

We covenant together to assure ministries and other services to persons with AIDS.... We ask for God's guidance that we might respond in ways that bear witness always to Jesus' own compassionate ministry of healing and reconciliation; and that to this end we might love one another and are for one another with the same unmeasured and unconditional love that Jesus embodied.*

Etta Mae: In the beginning of the HIV/AIDS pandemic, people feared for their own safety. No one wanted to come in contact with a death-dealing virus. The fear arose from unanswered questions about the origin of the disease, and it spread on the wings of untruths regarding the transmission of the virus.

Fearful people stigmatized those who were sick. Fearful people judged and condemned those living with AIDS. Fearful people paralyzed communities and blocked efforts to respond with care.

With HIV/AIDS the fear of disease mixed with prejudice against homosexual persons. In the United States, homosexual men were one of the first populations to contract the disease. Fearful and prejudiced people then began condemning gay men for causing the disease. In fact AIDS was originally transmitted through heterosexual contact in central Africa. That does not mean, however, that African people caused the disease. Any population, once exposed, will be affected.

Perhaps a fearful people may be excused for racing into panic. Certainly a fearful people may be led toward understanding through education. We have committed ourselves to that educational task.

Fritz: In 1992 I was elected to the office of Bishop in The United Methodist Church. The process is spiritual and political. The election takes place at a regional conference called the Jurisdictional Conference. We live and serve in the South Central Jurisdiction. Lay and clergy delegates are elected from each of the seventeen annual conferences from the states of Missouri, Arkansas, Louisiana, Nebraska, Kansas, Oklahoma, Texas, and New Mexico. Usually those elected have been nominated by their home conference. In my case the Missouri West Conference believed that I had the skills, experience, and spiritual wisdom to be considered for election. In fact, they had put forth my name in 1988 also.

This election process took place less than a year after Fred's death. Many people knew that two of our sons had died of AIDS. Some thought this disqualified me from consideration. When we first learned that Tim and Fred were gay, I met with a friend who was one of the delegates. I told him about their disclosure and invited his reflection. He suggested that I tell both Tim and Fred that homosexuality was a sin and that I could not accept their lifestyle. I responded that we did not believe that sexual orientation was a choice and that God surely would not condemn those who had no choice in the matter. That conversation confirmed my belief that I would be attacked and judged unfit for the episcopacy. I considered withdrawing from consideration.

The episcopal election procedure includes a personal interview with the delegations from all of the annual conferences. Several questions were asked about my stance. I responded by lifting up the statement in *The Book of Discipline*:

> Homosexual persons no less than heterosexual persons are individuals of sacred worth. All persons need the ministry and guidance of the church in their struggles for human fulfillment, as well as the spiritual and emotional care of a fellowship that enables reconciling relationships with God, with others, and with self. Although we do not condone the practice of homosexuality and consider this practice incompatible with Christian teaching, we affirm that God's grace is available to all. We commit ourselves to be in ministry for and with all persons.

I expressed my hope that we might focus on grace and avoid judgments. I advocated for a suspension of judgment since there is such disagreement over the cause and nature of homosexuality.

Many disagreed with my position, of course, but no one chose to attack me personally. In the end I was elected in spite of these differences. There is more to the exercise of episcopal spiritual leadership, after all, than dealing with official positions about homosexuality.

Etta Mae: Even so, dealing with prejudice is a very difficult matter. When prejudice is fanned long enough, it eventually evolves into hatred. After the election in July 1992, we moved to Topeka, Kansas. Before we arrived in late August, colleagues warned us about a church in Topeka that made hatred and condemnation the hallmark of their ministry. They warned us that this particular congregation focused on judgment against persons infected with AIDS, against homosexual persons.

This particular church engages in the "ministry" of picketing. Day after day, members of the congregation may be seen somewhere in the city, carrying disgusting placards that demean and slander persons. Churches, government offices, and civic institutions serve as targets. Often individuals are singled out. Their most distasteful practice, perhaps, is to picket the funerals of persons who have died of AIDS.

It took a few months, but we became the object of this blind hatred. A gang began to appear at conferences where Fritz spoke. They carried posters with the message, "FAG METHODIST CHURCH" and "FAG BISHOP MUTTI." As they waved their placards, they hurled vile epithats and deliberately tried to provoke angry responses.

Abuse like that hurts. The adage "words can never hurt you" is not true. Hatred hurts. It stings to the core. It brings out anger that you never knew was inside you.

We know of very few people outside that one church who defend such shameful behavior. Yet over and over again we feel the same kind of hostility from otherwise upstanding church members. "It is the sin we hate," they say. "We love persons with AIDS. We love homosexual persons. It is the sin we hate."

The use of the word "hate" reveals the underlying message.

That certainly is the feeling we perceive. That word "hate" hides entirely the loving intention.

Still, fearful people can come to understanding; condemning people can become caring people. The love of Jesus Christ changes our hearts and mends our ways. Because Jesus first loved us, we begin to love others. When we love others, we stand with them in their need. We suffer with those who suffer. We encourage those who have lost hope. We believe that life triumphs over death.

Fritz: Vast numbers now enter the struggle against judgment and hatred. World AIDS Day marks the occasion when millions pause to remember those who suffer and those who labor toward the day when HIV is destroyed.

The week of World AIDS Day in 1993, I was invited to a White House Prayer Breakfast to discuss ways in which the wider community can mobilize a response to this terrible crisis. President Clinton and Vice President Gore listened to the fourteen of us invited guests tell our stories. Then the group explored possible courses of action. In some small way I may have made a contribution to the struggle for service and healing.

Now we continue to share our story, to teach and to stand as advocates for an open and inclusive church and society. We engage in the ongoing, and painful, dialogue that seeks understanding. We live with the tensions resultant from uncertainty about the causes and nature of homosexuality. It is a difficult and wearisome burden to carry. We keep at the task because we believe the Holy Spirit is at work in the dialogue. We do not claim a corner on the truth, but we believe that the church can err too.

During the United Methodist General Conference held in Denver in 1996, I was one of fifteen United Methodist bishops who signed a statement acknowledging that our personal convictions are contradicted by the proscriptions in the *Discipline* against gay and lesbian persons within our church. With my colleagues I urged United Methodist churches to open their doors in gracious hospitality to all our brothers and sisters in the faith. We pledged faithfully to administer the provisions of the *Discipline,* in spite of our personal beliefs.

A firestorm erupted after the statement was released. Hundreds of letters came to my desk, and I patiently answered every one that came from a church member in Kansas. Many denied that I could hold my personal convictions and enforce the rules of our Church at the same time. I confess the tension but still commit to the vows of my consecration.

* (From The United Methodist Church's Resolution "AIDS and the Healing Ministry of the Church," *The Book of Resolutions of The United Methodist Church* (Nashville: The United Methodist Publishing House, 1996), pp. 109-10.

26

FACING LIFE THROUGH FAITH

We come to the end of this book, but we are not at the end of the story. Life goes on for us and for everyone. We bear the pain of our ordeal and carry the scars of our loss.

We relived our anguish as we moved from chapter to chapter. Every day, as we sat at the keyboard composing, the memories forced up tears and sighs. Our pain is not resolved; it will never go away.

In spite of this, our hopes are stronger than ever. We look to the promises of God and claim them in our lives. We look to the community of faith and share our experience, our hopes, and our faith with other pilgrims in the journey.

We hope this book has conveyed something of the terror of this illness. We trust that you have ridden the ups and downs with us. Most of all we hope that we have shared enough of our faith that we now hold that faith together.

We now end this final chapter with a quotation and a prayer. The quotation comes from our friends Cathie Lyons and Don Messer:

The remarkable thing about love is that it is full of surprises. Every time we think we have a fix on it, the terrain shifts a bit as if to test us, to force a reality check on us, to make us look at it from a different angle, to see if it is really love at all.

In a sermon delivered on the subject of AIDS, Dr. Donald Messer, former president of Iliff Theological Seminary, included this statement about love:

> So in the end love comes down to this . . . not some Clark Gable appraisal of Vivien Leigh or some sex symbol's seductive pose, but "Help me sit up." In the end love is not a smoldering glance across the dance floor, the click of crystal, a leisurely picnic spread upon summer's clover. It is the squeeze of a hand. I'm here. I'll be here no matter how long the struggle. Water? You need water? Here. . . . Drink. . . . Let me straighten your pillow.

Dance floors are very good places to experience loving care. The bride took our son's hand, pulled him and his wheelchair onto the dance floor and they danced.

BENEDICTION

Loving God, you make yourself known to us in Jesus Christ, who is the Lord of the Dance. He meets us where we are: in our suffering, in our pain, in our struggle and commitment. He takes our hands and pulls us onto the dance floor.

Give us, through your Holy Spirit, grace to dance in our wheelchairs. Forgive us when we fear taking the risk. Encourage us when we are too tired. Strengthen us when we are too weak.

Lead us in the dance, we pray. Amen.